W9-ADG-404

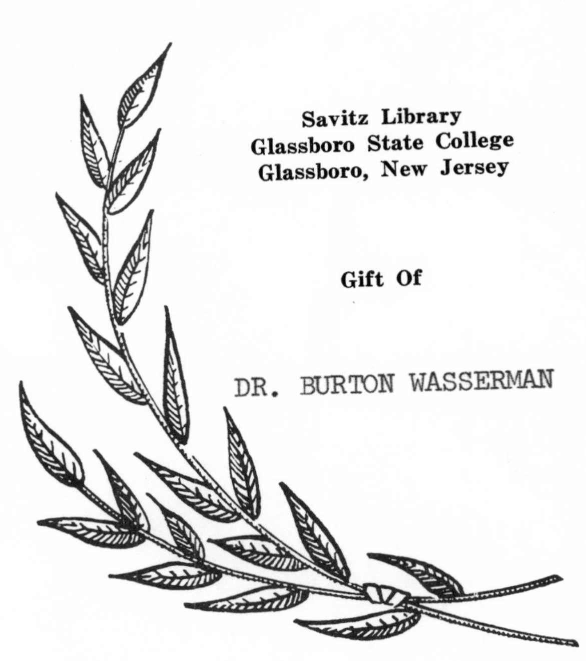

EARLY AMERICAN WEAVING AND DYEING

EARLY AMERICAN WEAVING AND DYEING

THE DOMESTIC MANUFACTURER'S ASSISTANT AND FAMILY DIRECTORY IN THE ARTS OF WEAVING AND DYEING

By J. and R. Bronson

With a New Introduction by
RITA J. ADROSKO
Curator, Division of Textiles
National Museum of History and Technology

DOVER PUBLICATIONS, INC.
NEW YORK

Published in Canada by General Publishing Company, Ltd., 30 Lesmill Road, Don Mills, Toronto, Ontario.

Published in the United Kingdom by Constable and Company, Ltd., 10 Orange Street, London WC2H 7EG.

This Dover edition, first published in 1977, is an unabridged and slightly corrected republication of the work originally published by William Williams in Utica, New York, in 1817 under the title, *The Domestic Manufacturer's Assistant and Family Directory in the Arts of Weaving and Dyeing*. Rita J. Adrosko has written a new Introduction especially for the Dover edition; and a list of Common Names of Chemicals Used in Dyeing is reprinted from *Natural Dyes and Home Dyeing*, by Rita J. Adrosko, New York, Dover Publications, Inc., 1971.

International Standard Book Number: 0-486-23440-1
Library of Congress Catalog Card Number: 76-26289

Manufactured in the United States of America
Dover Publications, Inc.
180 Varick Street
New York, N.Y. 10014

INTRODUCTION TO THE DOVER EDITION

The information that J. and R. Bronson recorded in their useful little volume is all that we know about these two men. Even "J.'s" relationship to "R." and his first name are unknown, although we assume that "R." is the Russel Bronson who had the dye section of this book reprinted in 1826.

The book was originally published in Utica, New York, in 1817 under the title *The Domestic Manufacturer's Assistant, and Family Directory, in the Arts of Weaving and Dyeing*. The fact that the dye section was reprinted suggests that at least that section of this publication was a success in its own time; the recommendation in 1818 by the president of the Berkshire Agricultural Society that "every housekeeper and manufacturer . . . purchase [the book] without delay" was apparently taken seriously by a number of people. It also suggests that the Bronsons' reduction of quantities in dye recipes and yarn calculations in weaving projects filled a need that previous books written for "practical dyers and manufacturers" had not achieved.

This latest reprinting by Dover Publications offers twentieth-century craftsmen a practical as well as a historical guide to hand-weaving patterns and dye recipes. Contemporary craftsmen are reminded that in the 159 years since the Bronsons' book first appeared some changes have been made in weaving equipment, in the purity of dye chemicals and in the quality of the dyestuffs themselves; some adaptations should be made, therefore, to make the information usable today.

The Weaving Drafts

The patterns in this book offer contemporary weavers with limited interest in historic textiles a fresh source of inspiration. For those interested in historic textiles, furthermore, the Bronsons' tables and calculations give a rough idea of the size and amount of yarn required for various projects, even if the figures cannot be taken literally in planning weaving projects. This information can be used as a guide to reproducing approximately the weaves and color combinations of a variety of fabrics used in the United States during the first quarter of the nineteenth century.

Without actual fabric samples showing color and texture, exact reproduction of these early fabrics is impossible. A close facsimile of early fabrics is possible when they are made of wool or linen, because these fibers can be handspun into a texture and size which resembles early handspun yarn. Cottons pose a greater problem, because the correct type and color of unmercerized cotton yarn would be much more difficult to obtain today.

The Bronsons' weave drafts are written for use with counterbalanced and countermarch looms, threaded right to left and back to front. Directions for countermarch looms mention "short lams" and "long lams." Mary Meigs Atwater (see below) recommends the use of a jack-type loom for Bronson weaves, which require the heavy use of one shaft. She has transposed some of these drafts for use on four shafts.

Here, where there is a special arrangement of numbers in a draft, like "$\begin{array}{ccccc} & 7 & & 1 & \\ 6 & & & & 2 \\ & 5 & & 3 & \\ & & 4 & & \end{array}$" in Pattern No. 1 (p. 54), their position in the arrangement is not significant. Each number should be followed in order for drawing-in (labeled "draft") and for treadling (labeled "treadles"). The tie-ups (labeled "cording") are a bit difficult to read. The +s indicate a lowered harness (shaft); the -¦-s indicate a raised harness (shaft). The "stars" mentioned in the text refer to these plus signs. The words "shaft," "harness," and "wing" are frequently interchangeable.

Pattern No. 1, for example, has seven yarns in its warp repeat. Its drawing-in order (draft) starting from the right is:

Warp 1 through the first heddle on harness A (the back harness)
Warp 2, harness B
Warp 3, harness C
Warp 4, harness D (the front harness)
Warp 5, harness C
Warp 6, harness B
Warp 7, harness A.

In the tie-up (cording):

harnesses A and D are tied to treadle E (the right treadle);
harnesses A and C, to treadle F
harnesses A and B, to treadle G
harnesses C and D, to treadle H (the left treadle).

The treadling order is:

treadle E is first
treadle H is second
treadle E is third
treadle G is fourth
treadle F is fifth
treadle H is sixth
treadle F is seventh
treadle G is eighth.

Of the thirty-five weaving patterns included, one utilizes 3 shafts; six are 4-shaft weaves; eight are 5-shaft weaves; eight are 6-shaft weaves; eleven are 8-shaft weaves; and one "damask diaper" uses 12 shafts.

The weaves which Mrs. Atwater classifies as "spot" or "Bronson" are among some of the 5-, 6- and 8-shaft weaves she found in the Bronsons' book. All the 5-shaft weaves are Atwater's "Bronson" weaves, as are 6-shaft weaves

9, 10, 19, 25 and the 8-shaft weave No. 28. Mrs. Atwater concluded that this weave had an English origin, because the only other place she was able to find it was in an old English weaving book, which incidentally referred to it as a "spot" weave. In England it had apparently been used for woolen shawls, while in America it was mainly used for linens. Mrs. Atwater felt that this weave could be applied by modern weavers where lace effects were desirable, and devoted a short section of *The Shuttle-Craft Book of American Hand-Weaving* to what she called the "Bronson" or "spot" weave (N.Y.: Macmillan, 1951, pp. 240–246).

The short glossary which follows translates some of the terms used by the Bronsons which are not in common use today.

Beer. Group of yarns which make up a section of the warp. The number of yarns in a beer varies. According to the *Oxford English Dictionary* a beer is known as a "porter" in Scotland. It is a name given to a variable number of ends (interlaced with a cord) into which a warp is divided in the process of warping, in order to facilitate the opening and dividing of the warp after sizing, while being wound on the beam; it also facilitates the subsequent process of weaving.

Bout. 48 warp threads (p. 36: "25 bouts or 50 half bouts . . . 1200 threads").

Broach. A spindle. See Copp.

Copp. Spun yarn wound on the spindle.

Cording. Tie-up.

Girth Beam. Crossbeam of a loom, located over the weaver's working area.

Harness. A term which the Bronsons use in referring to individual heddles (pp. 36–37), the heddles taken as a group (p. 38), or the whole set of shafts with connecting cords and other parts of the shedding system (p. 38). Many modern weavers use the word "harness" when referring to the unit which contains the heddles. This is also known as a "shaft." Also see WING.

HELVE. Heddle.

KNOT. Number of skeins of yarn wound off one full reel. One knot = 7 factory knotted skeins = 10 home-knotted skeins.

LAITH. Beater.

RAITH. Raddle.

RUN. Unit of measurement for the amount of yarn wound off a reel. 20 knots = one run.

SCALLET FRAME. Spool rack.

SHADE. Shed.

SKEIN. Length of thread or yarn wound in a coil; also the quantity of yarn wound off a reel. One skein = 10 knots.

SLAIE. A term used by the Bronsons in several ways. Sometimes it refers to the beater or reed (p. 38) or to the number of dents in the reed (charts on pp. 13–15) or the total number of groups of dents in the width of a reed (p. 30).

SPLIT. Dent of the reed. The Bronsons also refer to a dent as a "reed."

THRUM END. Warp beam end of the warp. According to the *Oxford English Dictionary* THRUM refers to each of the ends of the warp threads left unwoven and remaining attached to the loom when the web is cut off; usually used in the plural. The row or fringe of such threads, or a short piece of waste thread or yarn; the plural can also refer to odds and ends of thread.

THRUM ROD. Rod which is inserted through the THRUM END of the warp.

WARPING BARS. Warping board.

WEB. Piece of woven goods.

WIDTH. A yard was a standard width during the Bronsons' time. ¾ = ¾ yard (a common width for shirting); ⅞ = ⅞ yard (usual for bed ticking); 11/4 = 2¾ yards (broadcloth).

WING. Shaft. Commonly called a harness by modern hand-weavers.

The Dye Recipes

Before one attempts to use any of the recipes in this book, certain problems inherent in using early dye recipes should be recognized. Since the state of early nineteenth-century chemical manufacture was, by modern standards, primitive, dye chemicals used then were considerably less pure than those available today. Thus the potency of modern chemicals would differ enough so that proportions might have to be adjusted. Lack of standardization of modern natural dyestuffs would make the quantities stated merely rough estimates. Just as there were various grades of early dyestuffs, modern natural dyes such as madder may differ greatly from supplier to supplier, depending on whether or not they contain twigs or other natural adulterants which affect their potency.

There is no way of judging the standards by which early dyers measured the success of a dye job. While clear, even colors have been the goal of dyers of all eras, other standards for judging success of a dye job could have changed over the years. Modern dyers usually strive for soft, noncompacted products. It is quite possible that certain early woolens, for example, might have been considered desirable if firm and solid. Thus even if one succeeded in surmounting all other obstacles, following these dye recipes too literally could lead to results that could be considered unsatisfactory by present-day standards.

Certain of the Bronsons' recommendations, such as keeping knots and loops loose so that the dye can penetrate, are excellent. Other directions, such as entering wool into a pot of scalding hot water or stirring wool around, are less useful. Only those recommendations which agree with contemporary tested dye practices should be followed.

The amounts of dye materials, especially half-pounds of the main dyestuffs called for in many recipes, should be questioned. They might in many cases be wasteful of very expensive dyestuffs. Also, since cotton is much more difficult than wool to dye and the results may be colors with limited fastness, cotton dye recipes should be attempted first using experimental quantities.

If you wish to experiment with these recipes, it is advisable first to select a reliable modern book on the subject, which offers "how-to-do-it" instructions. Once you have tried a few recipes and feel you understand certain basic features, such as the usual proportions of mordants, dyestuffs and dye chemicals, and how and when they are used, you are ready to experiment with the Bronsons' recipes.

The list of "Common Names of Chemicals Used in Dyeing" included in this volume is reprinted from my book, *Natural Dyes and Home Dyeing* (New York: Dover, 1971). It will assist modern dyers in translating obsolete names of dye chemicals.

RITA J. ADROSKO

Washington, D.C.
July, 1976

Common Names of Chemicals Used in Dyeing**

Alum	Potassium aluminum sulfate	$KAl(SO_4)_2 \cdot 12\ H_2O$
Aqua ammonia	Ammonium hydroxide solution	NH_4OH
Aqua fortis	Nitric acid	HNO_3
Aqua regia	Mixture of HCl and HNO_3	$HCl + HNO_3$
Argol (Argal or Argil)	Crude potassium bitartrate, red or white, depending on whether it is deposited from red or white grapes	—
Bleaching powder	Calcium hypochlorite	$CaOCl_2$
Blue stone	Blue vitriol (below)	—
Blue vitriol	Hydrated copper sulfate	$CuSO_4 \cdot 5\ H_2O$
Borax	Hydrated sodium tetraborate	$Na_2B_4O_7 \cdot 10\ H_2O$
Brimstone	Sulfur	S
Caustic potash	Potassium hydroxide	KOH
Caustic soda	Sodium hydroxide	NaOH
Chalk	Calcium carbonate	$CaCO_3$
Chrome mordant	Potassium dichromate	$K_2Cr_2O_7$
Chrome yellow	Lead chromate	$PbCrO_4$
Cinnabar	Mercuric sulfide	HgS
Copperas	Hydrated ferrous sulfate	$FeSO_4 \cdot 7\ H_2O$
Cream of tartar	Potassium acid tartrate	$KHC_4H_4O_6$
Fuller's earth	Hydrated magnesium and aluminum silicates	—
Glycerine	Glycerol	$C_3H_5(OH)_3$
Green vitriol	Copperas (above)	—
Javelle water	Sodium hypochlorite solution	NaOCl
Lime water	Water solution of calcium hydroxide	$Ca(OH)_2 \cdot H_2O$
Lye	Caustic soda (above)	—
Marine acid	Muriatic acid (below)	—
Milk of lime	Calcium hydroxide suspended in water	$Ca(OH)_2$
Muriatic acid	Hydrochloric acid	HCl
Nitre	Potassium nitrate	KNO_3
Oil of vitriol	Concentrated sulfuric acid	H_2SO_4
Orpiment	Arsenic trisulfide	As_2S_3
Pearl ash	Purified potash (below)	K_2CO_3

**Chief reference: Francis M. Turner, ed., *The condensed chemical dictionary*, 2nd ed., rev. New York: The Chemical Catalog Co., Inc., 1930.

Peroxide	Hydrogen peroxide	H_2O_2
Potash	Potassium carbonate	K_2CO_3
Prussian blue	Ferric ferrocyanide	$Fe_4(Fe(CN)_6)_3$
Prussic acid	Hydrocyanic acid	HCN
Realgar	Arsenic monosulfide	AsS
Red orpiment	Arsenic bisulfide	As_2S_2
Sal ammoniac	Ammonium chloride	NH_4Cl
Sal soda	Hydrated sodium carbonate	$Na_2CO_3 \cdot 10\ H_2O$
Saleratus	Pearl ash overcharged with carbonic acid gas	—
Saltpetre	Nitre (above)	—
Sig	Urine, whose principal constituent is urea, a weakly basic nitrogenous compound	$CO(NH_2)_2$ (urea)
Slaked lime	Hydrated calcium hydroxide	$Ca(OH)_2$
Soda ash	Sodium carbonate	Na_2CO_3
Sour water	Dilute sulfuric acid	H_2SO_4
Spirit of salt	Muriatic acid (above)	—
Spirits of nitre	Dilute nitric acid	$HNO_3 \cdot H_2O$
Sugar of lead	Lead acetate	$Pb(C_2H_3O_2)_2 \cdot 3\ H_2O$
Tannic acid (tannin)	Gallotannic acid	$C_{14}H_{10}O_9$
Tartar	Argol (above)	—
Verdigris	Basic copper acetate	$CuO \cdot 2Cu(C_2H_3O_2)_2$
Vermillion	Cinnabar (above)	—
Vinegar	Dilute impure acetic acid	CH_3COOH
Vitriol	A sulfate, usually of iron or copper	—
Vitriolic acid	Oil of vitriol (above)	—
Washing soda	Sal soda (above)	—

THE

DOMESTIC MANUFACTURER'S ASSISTANT,

AND

FAMILY DIRECTORY,

IN THE ARTS

OF

WEAVING AND DYEING:

COMPREHENDING

A PLAIN SYSTEM OF DIRECTIONS,

APPLYING TO THOSE ARTS AND OTHER BRANCHES NEARLY CONNECTED WITH THEM IN THE MANUFACTURE OF

COTTON AND WOOLLEN GOODS;

INCLUDING MANY USEFUL

TABLES AND DRAFTS,

IN CALCULATING AND FORMING VARIOUS KINDS AND PATTERNS OF GOODS, DESIGNED FOR THE IMPROVEMENT OF DOMESTIC MANUFACTURES.

BY J. & R. BRONSON.

UTICA;

PRINTED BY WILLIAM WILLIAMS,

NO. 60, GENESEE STREET.

1817.

PREFACE.

THE arts of Weaving and Dyeing attracted our attention as early as the year 1800, and from that period until the present, our time has been chiefly occupied in those branches and others nearly connected therewith, and mostly in manufacturing establishments.

From these advantages and the assistance our manufacturing friends have obligingly afforded us, we feel satisfied that we possess competent means of information to publish a book of this kind, which we believe will prove valuable to Manufacturers of Cotton and Woollen goods, and particularly to those who wish to manufacture in their own families.

Its usefulness we trust will readily be acknowledged, being designed for the improvement of two important branches of manufacture, the practice of which we have attempted to explain in familiar terms, by a regular system in the various branches appertaining to dyeing and manufacturing of Cotton and Wool. The books which have been heretofore published on these branches, have generally been calculated only for practical Dyers and manufacturers, and although their instructions have generally been correct, yet they have often failed to afford immediate benefit to the inexperienced, by not descending to point out many minute particulars, which, to them, must be allowed highly necessary and essential. *To obviate* this difficulty, it has been our intention in this work, to express ourselves with plainness, and at the same time to note the most important points requisite to obtain good colors, and manufacture cloth to the best advantage.

On the subject of Cotton weaving we have given exact Tables and examples, which will be found very valuable in calculating and forming the various kinds of Plaids, Stripes, Checks, Shirting, Sheeting Ticking &c.

In this plan, plain directions are given to ascertain the exact length that any number of Skeins, runs or knots of yarn will warp, of the various widths and Slaies of Cotton goods now generally manufactured in our country.

PREFACE.

The tables and examples only, which we have given, will be found worth the price of the book to a great number of manufacturers, also to many that are or may be interested in manufacturing establishments, should they pay that attention to it which the subject demands.

We have endeavoured to explain and instruct on the subject of Woollen weaving, in the most approved method now practiced, and as this branch of household manufacture is more important and extensive than any other, we believe the improvements lately made in large Woollen factories which we have inserted, will be found very interesting.

On the art of Dyeing, it will be found we have given a greater variety of receipts, than will be found in any book extant for the same price; and when it is considered that it is seldom that a book has been published on Weaving and Dyeing both in one volume, we think many will avail themselves of an opportunity to procure such a work.

It is well known that many families wish to have Cotton and Woollen yarn, Flannels, Garments &c. dyed in that season of the year when clothiers cannot conveniently attend to it: this book to such will be a valuable acquisition, as also to many who are situated at a considerable distance from clothiers, who do not practice dyeing fancy colors such as Scarlet, Crimson and Madder-red on Wollen; also Red, Yellow, Green and Orange on Cotton. These colors may be dyed in families to advantage where the quantity is not large, which will be useful and ornamental in the manufacture of Carpeting, coverlets, Shawls, Net-work, Fringe, Plaids, Stripes &c.

We would not wish to be understood that families can dye all their cloth to advantage themselves, especially if the quantity is large, for in such cases it would require larger kettles than what are generally used for domestic purposes. In dyeing of Scarlet and other fancy colors on Woollen, and the various colors on cotton, we have given such particular and plain directions, that there will be no difficulty for any family to obtain them, should they follow the rules with exactness, which will be found indispensably necessary.

Of the merits of this work the public will judge: having no desire to raise our reputaion at the expense of those who have preceded us, and conscious that we have employed the means of information with patient industry and strict integrity in the execution of it, we are willing to abide the decision of those who examine for themselves and judge with candor

New-Hartford, Oneida Co.
N. Y. July, 1817.

INDEX.

ERRATA.

Page 25, 5th line from the top, for 80 skeins deep blue, read 64. 6th line for 32 skeins copperas color, read 32 skeins *pale blue,* also reckon 16 skeins of white.

30, bottom line, for No. 12, read No. 10.

36, 5th line from bottom, for no read *on.*

44, 6th line from top, for roke read *broke.*

46, 26th line from top, for thumb read *thrumb.*

52, 7th line from top, for put read *leave out.*

54, for stars, read *crosses.*

MANUFACTURER'S ASSISTANT.

Observations on Looms and utensils used in weaving.

DURING several years past, there has been many kinds of looms invented and offered to the public as improvements on the old constructed Fly Shuttle and hand loom. Some of these are operated in all parts (except shifting the temples, and bobbin or quill) by only moving the laith with the hands to and fro; some are operated by the same method in all parts, except the treading, which is done by the feet: others again the shuttle only is operated by the motion of the Laith.

These different kinds of Looms, are no doubt used to advantage for plain weaving, where they are used by patient and experienced weavers, who are willing and can to advantage, place their whole attention to keep their loom, and work in order; but if not so, it is very reasonable to suppose that the common Fly shuttle or hand loom, is to be preferred before the other kinds yet invented. It is certain that the Fly shuttle loom just spoken of, or the hand loom, will make better Cloth than the others described, especially when they are used by new beginners.

In making these remarks, we would not by any means wish to condemn those looms of a new and complicated construction, but only observe, that we think they are not so well calculated in general for common use: as it is found that unless a person is extremely careful in working such looms, they will damage the cloth.

In fact when we examine the looms in Cotton and Woollen Factories, both for twill and plain work, and find the old fashioned Fly shuttle loom still encouraged, we are led at once to believe that the old plan is better than any other yet adopted.

Some persons have supposed that by the use of the new constructed Loom, the labor in weaving is made more easy and light, by operating all the parts by the movement of the Laith: but this is a mistaken idea; for surely if all these movements are to be set at work by the strength of the hands and arms only, it must in the end prove more tiresome than to have the labour more equally distributed by the work of the hands and feet.

The common Fly shuttle Loom differs but little from the common hand loom, and that is in the laith, and shooting the shuttle. The Laith of the former one is moved with the left hand, while the other hand, by the help of a cord, jerks or drives the shuttle through the piece. This manner of weaving is more easy, and attended with less hard labor than that of the hand loom, in particular from this plan allowing you to set upright in the loom; whereas in weaving in the hand loom, you have to reach forward to throw the shuttle.

After speaking of the different kinds of looms we would remark that the Common Fly shuttle is to be preferred in some cases to the hand loom, that is, when the learner has instruction from a person well acquainted with that kind of weaving, or from an ingenious and good weaver in the common loom.

Cording of Looms.

It is important that all the cords belonging to a Loom should be made very well, and of so large a size as to be strong. Many persons who weave occasionally in families, are not particular to make their cords well; in that case they fail very soon, besides often damaging the cloth by their giving way. Whereas if they would take a little more time in making them, they would wear a considerable length of time and save the weaver a great deal of unnecessary trouble.

Harness.

The twine for the harness of a loom should be made of good and well chosen Cotton or Linen yarn, and very evenly doubled and twisted. The wings or harness should without fail be dressed or starched well, with good brushes before weaving each piece, and in the manner as you will find among the instructions in Beaming and setting a piece to work. By paying attention to the harness in that respect, much time and expense will be saved in making new ones often. Those who have not practiced starching the harness, by making a beginning, will find by this practice, their trouble well compensated

---

Raith or Raddle.

The Raddle is thought by some to be an implement of no great consequence, as it respects its being made in a nice and workmanlike manner; but it is far otherwise. The weavers Raith or Raddle, should be made smooth, and the teeth set nice and tight, in order that the piece while beaming, may be spread even and in a proper manner: the expense of a good one is but trifling, and is an article that will last with good usage, a great length of time.

Temples.

This implement in weaving is too often made in a slighty manner, especially the points or teeth. The points or teeth should be made of hardened wire, of a suitable size, set even and near together, and filed very smooth.

Shuttle.

Shuttles should be made of fine grained hard wood, and of such a kind as will not incline to get rough in using.

Spools.

The spools for winding warp should be all of a size, so that in warping a piece they will turn alike and easy. It is also necessary that the sticks which the spools run on, should be straight and smooth which if so, will often admit the yarn to be warped without breaking a thread.

After making these observations on the different utensils used in weaving, it will not be improper to remark, that the quality and beauty of a piece of cloth is often injured, by using even one of the above utensils where it is badly made or out of repair.

A TABLE,

Of various Numbers of Cotton Yarn and Slaies; with the number of Knots required to warp a yard in length. For Cloth three quarters wide.

No of Yarn.		*No of Slaie.*		*Knots.*	
No 8	goes in a	32	and requires	12	to warp a yard.
9		34		13	
10		36		13½	
11		38		14	
12		40		15	
13		42		16	
14		44		16½	
15		44		16½	
16		46		17	
17		48		18	
18		50		19	
19		50		19	
20		52		19½	
21		54		20	
22		56		21	
23		56		21	
24		58		22	
25		58		22	
26		60		22½	
27		62		23	
28		64		24	
29		66		25	
30		68		25½	

The yarn in the above table, is calculated to fill a Slaie three quarters full; for instance a Slaie of 40 beers wide is to be filled 30 beers. N. B. By so many knots to warp a yard, means that the Factory 7 knotted skeins are 10 knots, as they are so in reality; being more threads in each tie, than those from family reels: each factory skein being in all our calculations reckoned ten knots or half a run. To cast the number of knots to warp a yard of cloth three quarters wide, take out one quarter of the beer, and halve the remainder. For example, in a 40 slaie one quarter out leaves 30, half of which is 15, knots to warp a yard.

Table of numbers of Cotton Yarn and Slaies, with the number of knots required to warp a yard in length.

FOR CLOTH ONE YARD WIDE.

No of Yarn.		*No of Slaie.*		*Knots*	
No 8	goes in a	32	and requires	16	to warp a yard.
9		34		17	
10		36		18	
11		38		19	
12		40		20	
13		42		21	
14		44		22	
15		44		22	
16		46		23	
17		48		24	
18		50		25	
19		50		25	
20		52		26	
21		54		27	
22		56		28	
23		56		28	
24		58		29	
25		58		29	
26		60		30	
27		62		31	
28		64		32	
29		66		33	
30		68		34	

The yarn in the above table is calculated to fill a slaie full; and observe, it requires half as many knots to warp a yard of cloth one yard wide, as there are beers in the slaie. For instance, No. 12 yarn in a 40 slaie 1 yard wide, requires 20 knots or 2 skeins to warp 1 yard in length. For example, you wish to calculate for 60 yards of cloth, thus: 20) 120 (60 yards.

120

Table of Yarn and Slaies; with the number of knots required to warp a yard in length. For Cotton Shirting three quarters wide when bleached.

No of Yarn.		*No of Slaie.*		*Knots*	
No 8	goes in a	32	and requires	13	to warp a yard
9		34		14	
10		36		15	
11		38		16	
12		40		17	
13		42		18	
14		44		19	
15		44		19	
16		46		20	
17		48		20	
18		50		21	
19		50		21	
20		52		22	
21		54		23	
22		56		24	
23		56		24	
24		58		25	
25		58		25	
26		60		26	
27		62		26	
28		64		27	
29		66		28	
30		68		29	

The following rule will answer to make out pieces or webs of ¾ shirting of any length, from the above table.

First set down the number of knots to warp a yard, thus, for example, in a 40 slaie—

17 knots to warp a yard,
60 yards you wish,

102

102,0 knots or 102 skeins.

Proof, 17) 102 0 (60 yards,
102

Method of calculating and forming the pattern or figure of any kind of Check, Plaid or stripe; which plan also ascertains the length of the piece and number of spools required, according to the figure.

In the first place determine what figure you will have, which you can choose according to your own fancy, or by copying after any sample of Plaid or stripe Gingham, or check in Handkerchief's. For example, you make choice of the following pattern, which is formed of 3 colors in the warp. Say take No. 12 Yarn for a 40 Slaie $\frac{3}{4}$ wide:—

8 threads of Deep Blue.
6 threads of Pale Blue.
2 threads of White.
16

making sixteen threads in the figure, observing that should more than one colour be used in the filling, it will form a Plaid; but if only one colour in the filling, it forms a stripe. The weaver must warp with spools, in proportion to the number of threads in the figure. For instance, take either the same number of spools as there are threads in the figure, twice the number, three times the number, and so on, according to the length you wish to have the piece. For example in this piece, take twice the number, with 3 skeins on a spool, which will make 32 spools, being

16 spools of Deep Blue
12 ——— of Pale Blue
4 ——— of White.
32

Thirty two spools with three skeins on a spool make 96 skeins: then by multiplying the number of skeins by 10, which we call the number of knots in a skein, gives the whole number of knots in 96 skeins, which is 960 knots, and you will find by cutting off the right hand cypher it will shew again the number of skeins.—Thus 96,0. You will find by examining the Tables of Yarn and Slaies, that it requires 15 knots to warp a yard of Cloth $\frac{3}{4}$ wide, of Yarn No. 12 in a 40 Slaie. By dividing 960 knots by 15 shews the length or number of yards there is in this piece, which you will find is 64.

Statement 32 spools
3 skeins on a spool
96 skeins
10 knots in a skein
96,0

knots to warp a yd. 15) 96,0 (64 Yards.

To find the exact number of skeins of the different colors which will be required, you must first state the whole number of skeins you have in this piece, which is 96: then divide them by the number of threads in the figure, which is 16; thus, how many times 16 are there in 96, answer 6; then multiply the threads of each color by 6, which shews the exact number of skeins of each kind of color. By this method you can calculate for any figure. For example thus :—

Figure in the warp.

	Deep Blue	*Pale Blue*	*White*
Threads—	8	6	2
	6 times		

is 48 Skeins of Deep Blue
is 36 Pale Blue
is 12 White

Knots to 15) 960
warp a yd.) 64 yards.

Figure in the Filling.

	D. Blue.	*P. Blue.*
Threads	8	6
	7 times	

is 56 Sk'ns D. Blue
is 42 P. Blue
98

96 Skeins of Warp No. 12.
98 of Filling No. 12.

From the above statement, you will find the whole form of it as the piece stands made out.

Filling Calculation.

In calculating the number of skeins of Filling which you will want to fill a piece, you must first state the number of threads that form the figure; then multiply by any number that will produce as many or a few more skeins than there is of warp—this method you will find produces an exact proportion of each color. The multiplier will be governed by the number of threads that form the figure. For instance; you choose a different figure in the filling than was stated for the piece you have made out, thus—

	D. Blue	*P. Blue*
Threads	4	4
	12 times	
is	48 Skeins of Deep Blue	
is	48	Pale Blue
	96	

After a piece or web is made out and ready for the weaver, if you wish to proceed regular you will have a direction attached to each piece, when made out. The following direction is calculated for the piece of Plaid you have made out.

Lay this for 64 yards of Cloth, in a 40 Slaie, make the Check,

In the Warp,	*In the Filling,*
8 threads of D. Blue	8 threads of D. Blue
6 do Pale Blue	6 do P. Blue
2 do White	

96 Skeins Warp, } No. 12, 32 Spools, wind 3 skeins
98 Filling. } on a spool.

Examples of Figures of various kinds in Cloth.

We shall now give directions to make a variety of figures or patterns, in Plaids, Stripes and Checks: also give some examples in making out Sheeting, Shirting, and Bed Ticking.

By a little study the learner will soon find out the plan, or principle on which any figure is formed. Those that are here made out, may be applied to any Slaie, only to take the right number of yarn and knots to warp a yard, as suited to it. After becoming acquainted with the rule of forming Plaids, Stripes, &c. it will be perceived that an innumerable and almost endless variety of patterns or figures, can be obtained with the greatest ease, and must be considered an object quite interesting and important to those concerned in Cotton Factories, and also to those who manufacture cotton cloth in families.

N. B. Observe when the different colored threads that form the figure are multiplied, you must reckon all that are of one color at a time, as you will find that in some figures, one color is placed in two or three separate positions; in which case you must reckon them all at a time, the same as you will find in some of the following examples in Plaids and Ticking.

Calculations in making out pieces or webs of cotton.

For a piece of Shirting $\frac{3}{4}$ wide, in a 38 Slaie. Yarn No. 11

Statement 16 Knots to warp a yard
60 Yards are wanted

knots to 16) 960 knots (60 yards
warp a yd.) 96

96 Skeins of warp, 24 Spools wind 4 Skeins on a
96 do of Filling. Spool.

By the rule just stated, it will be found that the number of knots to warp a yard are first noted; the knots are then multiplied by the number of yards you wish, which brings the number of skeins required. The whole number of skeins or knots, are then divided by the number of knots to warp a yard; the quotient at the right then shews the number of yards of Cloth in the piece. In the above piece it requires 960 knots, which by cutting off the right hand cypher shews the number of skeins, which is 96.

For a piece of sheeting one yard wide, Calculated for yarn No. 12 in a 40 Slaie.

Rule 20 knots to warp a yard
60 yards are wished

knots to warp a yard) 20) 1200 (60 yards
120
120 Skeins of Warp
120 Filling.

30 Spools, with 4 skeins on a spool.

For a piece of stripe ¾ wide, Yarn No. 12 in a 40 Slaie.

Figure in the warp.

	Blue	*White*
threads	2	2

20 times

is 40 skeins of Blue
is 40 do White.

Filling.
80 skeins of 1 color.

15) 800 (53 yards
75
50
45
5

80 Skeins of warp.
80 do Filling.

20 spools, wind four Skeins on a spool.

N. B. In first multiplying the threads, you must observe that it is necessary to take an even number to multiply with. In varying it you will find it will produce more or less number of yards.

For a piece of Stripe ¾ wide, Yarn No. 13, *in a* 42 *Slaie.*

Figure in the Warp.

	Blue.	*White.*	
Threads,	4	2	
	16 times,		*Filling.*
	is 64 skeins of Blue.		[96 skeins of 1 color.]
	is 32 ,, White.		

Knots to warp a yard, 16) 96,0 (60 yards,
96
00

32 spools with 3 sk's on a spool
or 24 spools, with 4 on a spool.

96 skeins warp.
96 " filling

For a piece of Chambray, ¾ wide, Yarn No. 12, *in a* 40 *Slaie.*

Rule. 15 knots to warp a yard.
60 yards are wished.
00
90

Filling.
90 skeins of blue or any [other color.

knots w'p y'd 15) 900 (60 yards.
90

90 skeins of white warp.

30 spools, wind 3 skeins on a spool.

Chambray is made from any one color, as you wish, in the warp, and also in the filling; only have them differ from each other.

For Chambray ¾ wide, Yarn No. 16, in a 46 Slaie.

Rule. 17 knots to warp a yard.
60 yards are wished.

102

Filling.
102 skeins of blue or any [other color.

knots w'p y'd 17) 102,0 (60 yards
102

102 skeins of white warp.
34 spools, wind 3 skeins on a spool.

For a piece of Plaid ¾ wide, Yarn No. 12, in a 40 slaie.

	Figure in the Warp.		Figure in the Filling.	
	D. Blue.	*White.*	*Blue.*	*Copperas.*
threads	12	2	12	2
	6 times		6 times	
	is 72 skeins D. Bl.		is 72 skeins of Blue.	
	is 12 „ White,		is 13 „ of Copperas.	

knots w'p a yard 15)840(56 yards   84
75
90
90   28 spools, wind 3 skeins on a spool.

84 skeins warp.
84 „ filling.

For Plaid ¾ wide, Yarn No. 16, in a 46 Slaie.

Figure in the Warp.
D. Blue. White.

Threads 10 1
8 times.

is 80 skeins of Dark Blue.
is 8 „ of White.

knots to warp a 17) 88,0(51½ yards.
[yard, 85

30 22 spools, wind 4 skeins
17 [on a spool.

13

88 skeins of warp.
90 „ filling.

Figure in the Filling
D. Blue. Copperas.
10 2
7½ times.

is 75 skeins of Deep Blue.
is 15 of Copperas.

90

For Plaid ¾ wide, Yarn No. 13 in a 42 Slaie.

Figure in the Warp
P. Blue. Orange. D. Blue.
Threads 6 1 3
8 times

is 48 Skeins P. Blue
is 8 do Orange
is 24 do D. Blue

Figure in the Filling.
P. Blue. D. Blue.
8 4
7 times

is 56 Sk. P. Blue.
is 28 do D. Blue.

84

Knots to 16) 80 (50 yards
warp a yd. 80
80 Skeins of Warp.
84 do Filling.

20 Spools, wind 4 Skeins on a Spool.

For Plaid ¾ wide, Yarn No. 18 *or* 19, *in a* 50 *Slaie.*

Figure in the warp.

	D. Blue.	*P. Blue.*	*White.*
Threads	8	5	1

8 times.

is 64 skeins of Deep Blue.
is 40 skeins of Pale Blue.
is 8 skeins of white.

knots to warp a y'd. 19) 112,0 (59 yards.
95
170
152
18

Figure in the Filling.

D. Blue.	*Copperas.*
8	8

7 times.

is 56 skeins of Deep Blue.
is 56 skeins of Pale Blue.
112

28 spools, wind 4 skeins on a spool.

112 skeins of warp.
112 skeins of filling.

For Plaid ¾ wide, Yarn No. 21, *in a* 54 *Slaie.*

Figure of the Filling.

D. Blue.	*Copperas.*
10	2

9½ times.

is 95 skeins Deep Blue.
is 19 skeins Copperas Color.
114

Figure in the Warp.

	D. Blue.	*P. Blue.*	*White.*	*P. Blue.*
threads,	8	2	2	2
	8 times.			

is 80 skeins Deep Blue.
is 32 skeins Copperas Color.

knots warp a yard 20) 112,0 (56 yards.
100
120
120

112 skeins of warp.
114 skeins of filling.

28 spools, wind 4 skeins on a spool.

For Plaid ¾ wide, Yarn No. 16, *in a* 46 *slaie.*

Figure in the warp.

	D. Blue.	*Cop.*	*D. Blue.*	*Cop.*
threads	10	2	2	2
	6 times.			

is 72 skeins of Deep Blue.
is 24 skeins of Copperas.

knots to w'p 17) 96,0 (56½ yards.
85
110
102
8

32 spools, wind 3 sk's on a spool

Figure in the Filling.

D. Blue.	*P. Blue.*	*D. Blue.*	*P. Blue.*
10	2	2	2
6 times.			

is 72 skeins of Deep Blue.
is 24 skeins of Pale Blue.

96

96 skeins of warp.
96 skeins of filling.

For Plaid ¾ wide. Yarn No. 17, in a 48 Slaie.

	Figure in the Warp.				Figure in the Filling.	
	D. Blue.	*P. Blue.*	*White.*	*Orange.*	*D. Blue*	*P. Blue.*
Threads	6	6	1	1	6	6
	8 times				$9\frac{1}{2}$ times	

is 48 Skeins D. Blue.
is 48 do P. Blue
is 8 do White
is 8 do Orange

is 57 Sk. D. B.
is 57 do P. B.
114

knots to 18) 112,0 (62 yards
warp a yd. 108
40
36
4

112 Skeins of Warp.
114 do of Filling

28 Spools, wind 4 Skeins on a Spool.

For Plaid ¾ wide. Yarn No. 16, in a 46 Slaie.

Figure in the Warp.

	D. Blue.	*White.*	*D. Blue.*	*White.*	*D. Blue.*	*White.*
Threads	8	1	1	1	1	1
	8 times					

is 80 Skeins Deep Blue
is 24 do of White

knots 17) 104,0 (61 yards
warp a yd. 102
20
17
3

104 Skeins of Warp
102 do of Filling

26 Spools, wind 4 Skeins on a Spool.

Figure in the Filling.

D. Blue.	*White.*	*D. Blue.*	*White.*	*D. Blue.*	*White.*
12	1	1	1	1	1

6 times

is 84 Skeins D. Blue
is 18 do White

102

For Plaid ¾ wide. Yarn No. 17, *in a* 48 *Slaie*

Figure in the Warp.

	D. Blue.	*White.*	*Green.*	*White.*
Threads	12	1	6	1

6 times

is 72 Skeins of Deep Blue
is 12 do of White
is 36 do of Green
knots to 18) 120,0 (66 2-3 yards
warp a yd. 108

120
108

12

Figure in the Filling.

D. Blue.	*Red.*	*P. Blue.*	*Red.*
12	2	6	2

5½ times

is 66 Skeins Deep Blue
is 22 do Red
is 33 do Pale Blue

121

120 Skeins of Warp
121 do Filling 20 Spools, with 6 skeins on a spool, or 40 Spools, with three on a spool.

For Plaid ¾ wide, Yarn No. 18, in a 50 Slaie.

Figure in the Warp.

	D. Blue.	*P. Blue.*	*White.*	*P. Blue.*
Threads	12	6	1	6

4 times

is 48 Skeins of Deep Blue
is 48 do of Pale Blue
is 4 do of White

knots to 19) 100,0 (52 2-3 yards
warp a yd. 95

50
38

12

Figure in the Filling.

D. Blue.	*P. Blue.*	*Cop.*	*P. Blue.*
12	6	2	6

4

is 48 Skeins of Deep Blue
is 48 do of Pale Blue
is 8 do of Copperas

104

100 Skeins Warp
104 Filling

25 spools, wind 4 skeins on a spool.

For Plaid ¾ wide. No. 22 or 23 in a 56 Slaie.

	Figure in the warp				Figure in the Filling.	
	D. Blue	*Orange*	*P. Blue*	*Orange.*	*D. Blue*	*P. Blue*
threads	6	2	8	2	6	6

6 times (warp) — 9 times (filling)

is 36 skeins of Deep Blue
is 48 do of Pale Blue
is 24 do of Orange

is 54 skeins D. Blue
is 54 do Pale Blue.
108

kts. 21) 108,0 (51 yards
to wp. a 105
yard.
30
21
9

108 Skeins Warp
108 do Filling

36 Spools, wind 3 skeins on a spool.

For a piece of Apron Check ¾ wide, Yarn No. 12, in a 40 Slaie

Figure in the Warp.

Blue. *White.*
threads 4 4
12 times,

is 48 skeins of Blue
is 48 White

knots warp a yd. 15) 960 (64 yards
90
60
60

Figure in the Filling.

Blue *White*
4 4
12 times

is 48 skeins of Blue.
is 48 of White.
96

96 skeins warp
96 filling

32 spools, wind 3 skeins on a spool, or 24 with 4 each

For a piece of Apron Check, 1 *Yard No.* 16, *in a* 46 *Slaie.*

Figure in the Warp.

Blue White

threads 6 6

12 times

is 72 skeins of Blue.

is 72 of White.

knots to a yard 23) 144,0 (62½ yards.

138

60

46

14

Figure in the Filling.

Blue. White.

6 6

12 times.

is 72 skeins of Blue.

is 72 White.

144

144 skeins of warp. 36 spools, wind 4 skeins

144 filling. [on a spool.

For Twilled Bed Ticking 7-8 *wide, Yarn No.* 11 *or* 12 *in the Warp...calculated for a* 36 *Slaie: to be drawn* 4 *threads in a split.*

Figure in the Warp.

White. Blue. White. Blue. White. Blue.

threads 16 2 2 6 2 2

5½ times. *Filling.*

110 skeins of white. 121 skeins white Filling

55 skeins of blue. [No. 10.

k's to 30) 165,0 (56 yards.

a y'd] 150 30 spools wind 5½ skeins on a spool.

150 165 skeins of warp. No. 11

150 121 filling. No. 12

The preceding piece is to be warped 56 yards, but will not be more than about 52 from the loom; which makes 4 tick patterns of 13 yards each. It is calculated to be drawn 32 beers wide, and to be wove with 4 treadles, and 4 wings.

Twilled Bed Ticking 7-8 wide, warp No. 9 or 10, in a 36 slaie: to be drawn 3 threads in a split.

Figure same the other in the Warp.

84 skeins of white.
42 skeins of blue.

knots to warp 22,5)126,0 (56 yds. or 52 yds. out of the
a yard 112 5 [loom.

1350 *Filling.*
1350 95 sk's white filling No. 8.

126 skeins of warp No. 10.
95 filling No. 8.

30 spools, wind 4 skeins and 2 factory ties on a spool

For a piece of Bed Ticking, wove the same as plain cloth but of a handsome figure, 7-8 wide, Yarn No. 10. in the warp, calculated for a 36 slaie, 2 threads in a split.

Figure in the Warp.

	White.	*Blue.*	*White.*	*Blue.*	*White.*	*Blue.*
threads	16	2	2	6	2	2

2 times

is 40 skeins white *Filling.*
is 20 skeins blue. 56 skeins white filling No 8

k's to a 16)60,0 (37½ yards.
yard 48

120 30 spools, wind 2 skeins on a spool
112 60 skeins warp No. 10.
8 56 skeins filling No. 8.

N. B. The above is calculated for 3 patterns.

GENERAL OBSERVATIONS,

On preparing Cotton Yarn for Weaving: which includes Sizing, Drying, Winding, Warping, Beaming, &c.

Before we attempt to explain and direct as to the manner of preparing cotton yarn for weaving, through the various operations, we must offer an apology to the experienced weaver who may happen to look over our pages, for the simplicity of the language we make use of: but when it is considered, that our general intention has been to introduce a practical work, adapted to the inexperienced, as well as those that have only a partial knowledge of the arts we treat of, we indulge a hope that no material disadvantage will arise from the course we have pursued, as most of our readers who are experienced in the different subjects, will easily understand them.

Sizing Cotton Yarn. For 20 pounds.

The first object in preparing cotton yarn for weaving is that of Sizing, which should be done in the following manner.

Put in a large wooden bowl, or other vessel, about two pounds of wheat flour; then add cold water and stir it continually, using as much water as will reduce it to a fine paste: then afterwards use more cold water gradually until it is thin enough to strain through a common sieve.

Now place a kettle over a fire with a sufficient quantity of water to wet the yarn; bring it to a scalding heat, then pour the cold size through a sieve into the kettle, and let it boil two or three minutes stirring it well.

Another kettle or tub should be ready, to use for working the yarn in the size. There are different methods used to handle the yarn in the size, but we have generally practiced the following, which is done by making the yarn into a chain. First take about 3 skeins of yarn, and place them together at whole length: then take 3 more and pass through the first, and double the last: then 3 more is to be put through the two loops of the last, and so on until you have prepared half of the yarn. Should you have 20 pounds in the whole, you will next make another chain the same as the other. After both chains are made, then tie the last two loops of each chain with a string.

In the next place put half of the yarn into an empty kettle or tub, by curling it round on the bottom of it and so on towards the top ; then stir your sizing and pour half of it on the yarn, when it is nearly scalding hot, then pound it moderately with a smooth stick a few minutes, then turn it over and work it together as before. Add the remainder of the yarn to the rest, put in as before, and pour on the remainder of thesizing, and work it together the same as the first parcel.

When the size has cooled a little so that you can endure to wring it with the hands, then wring out three skeins at a time, or one link, until it is all wrung.—Should you wish to be certain how hard it ought to be wrung, you can determine that point by drying at first three skeins ; this is on the supposition that you are not skilled in sizing yarn.

The reader perhaps will believe we are giving small and unimportant information ; but we earnestly solicit his patience until the piece is ready for weaving, and if he has practiced directions less particular heretofore, perhaps the methods here pointed out, when practiced, may convince him that particular rules are necessary.

Drying Sized Yarn.

After the yarn is properly wrung, it should be hung on smooth poles, in the following manner :—

Open the bunches, shake 2 or 3 of them on the hands lightly and hang them the whole length on the poles, far enough apart when spread to fill them ; and when these bunches are parted into skeins, they should be so far from each other that 5 pounds will require 2 poles of 8 feet in length. The yarn being now divided, begin by opening the ties of the skein flat, and then snap and strain it a little on the pole, keeping the skein thin and flat : so proceed with all the skeins.

Dry them in the warm weather out of doors in open air, but in winter in a warm room, as freezing will injure the sizing materially. By following the above directions, you will be able to wind the finest yarn with ease.

Winding the Yarn.

This is a simple operation, but it is easy to perplex the warper by conducting it in a careless manner. This branch is generally performed as it properly should be by small children, that expense may be saved, and they frequently run the yarn on in bunches, in a promiscuous manner ; this, as we have just observed, has a bad effect in warping. In fact, if it is wound on the spools carlessly it has a bad effect even in weaving the piece. Children should be taught to begin at one end of the spool and wind evenly to the other, and so backwards and forwards until finished. Tehere is even an advantage to the winder in paying attntion to this, as when the thread breaks, he knows at once where to look for it.

Warping.

To perform this branch well, it is necessary that the spools should all be of a size, and that the sticks which they turn upon be straight and smooth. It is in vain for us to attempt to manufacture cloths with neatness, if we neglect to provide utensils that are made in a proper manner, as we often find that by using even one implement that is not in order, it will materially injure the whole work.

For an example in warping, you will take 24 spools with 4 skeins on a spool; calculated for 60 yards of shirting No 11, which you will find stated in the calculations to make out pieces—place them on the scallet frame in two tiers, having the first spool on the lower division of sticks, 2 or 3 inches farther to the right than the first spool of the upper row, and so on with the rest. You must observe to have the yarn ends on the right hand side of the spools, as you stand facing the frame.

Next collect all the ends and tie a knot in them; then draw the threads straight, and put your right hand through the division of threads close up to the knot, then put your left hand thumb in the opening, placing the ball of the thumb close to the knot.

Next form the lease with your right hand, beginning to collect the threads about the same distance as the pins on the bars are from your left hand. First take the lower thread on the bottom division, being under side of your right hand and over the thumb; next of the upper division, upper side of your hand and under your thumb, and so on until you have taken up all the threads. The new beginner ought to count the threads as he takes them, otherwise there will be room to err. The lease will then be laid on the pins on the top of the bars or mill, just as you have it in your right hand, by parting the lease between the right and left hand, up to the knot on the end of the piece. Should you use a warping mill, you will now turn it round with the sun until you warp 60 yards, which is the length; 96 skeins will make $\frac{3}{4}$ of a yard wide, when wove and bleached.

Should you use the common warping bars, you will warp backwards and forwards, running the yarn from one pin to the other downwards, until you get 60 yards. In either manner of warping, when you get the length that is desired; cross the bouts on the bottom pins, then proceed back again, when you will again take the lease as before, and lay it on the two lease pins and carry the branches on to the farther pin and cross them; still saving the lease in the hand to put on the pins again. You will then proceed again as before, backwards and forwards, until you get 25 bouts or 50 half bouts, being 1200 threads.

In the next place secure the lease by tying a string through each part of it two or three times, and tie the end of the piece at the bottom of the bars in a similar manner—then take the piece off from the bars, taking the lease off first; beginning as follows:—Put your arm through the loop that was formed between the pins, then draw with the arm the piece a little way through that loop, which forms another; through which with the other, hand you form another and so on until you finish it, ready for beaming.

Harness.

It is necessary that the harness should be starched or dressed before weaving each piece, which is done in the following manner. Fix a strong cord with a weight to it no the bottom cords, that lead from the harness downwards, so that one harness will be single as it hangs in the loom.

Take 2 eggs and as much in quantity of wheat-flour starch, newly made but cold, and beat them well together. Should the harness be made of cotton,, which is the best for weaving of cotton, you will do well in that case to add to your starch a tea spoonful of melted glue, then beat it well together and brush the harness with it evenly for some time; taking care not to get it very wet. Now change the clasps if you use that kind of harness, and brush it over again, then put a rod in each parting next to the eye and let them remain until dry with the weight on.— When it is dry, change the weight to another one, and so on: after which hang them out of the way.

Beaming.

First take the warped piece and lay it on the floor under the yarn beam; then take the thrum end and carry it under the cloth beam, over the breast beam, and through the lathe: put through the thrum rod and secure it, then place the bouts in the raddle about 32 or 33 inches wide, for $\frac{3}{4}$ shirting, being about 5 inches wider than it will be when wove.

You will now place the thrum rod and yarn at an equal distance from each end of the beam or posts, and proceed to wind the yarn hard on the beam, keeping it perfectly smooth and free from ridges. As a remedy against ridges, move the raith or raddle moderately backwards and forwards at different periods in the course of beaming. The person who holds the yarn while beaming, should not let it slip through his hands but should go hand over hand once in a foot, and strike it occasionally, minding not to let it twist between his hands, and so proceed until it is all wound on.

The top of the beamed piece should be about the same width that it will be in the reed.

Drawing through the harness.

Most persons who have been accustomed to use

both the 2 and 4 shaft harness for plain cloth, prefer the latter; and we think it is much the best, as it divides the piece into 4 parts, and causes it to spring with more ease, and is less liable to break threads. For a person who has never seen this kind of harness in operation for plain work, it would be more difficult to keep it in order than the 2 shaft harness, but by weaving one or two pieces, the difficulty would be removed.

The four shafts being placed of an equal height, you will then hang the raith or raddle level, and so high as to have the lease 2 or 3 inches above the eyes or clasps in the harness.

In the next place put the rods through the lease, and fasten the rods at the end with a string; then cut the string that secures the lease, and also the thrums: then knot up, and it is ready for drawing through the harness.

First begin to draw the threads through at the right hand, thus—

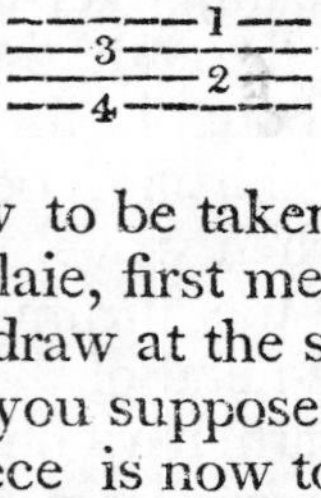

```
——3——1——
————————
————2———
——4—————
```

and so on through the whole piece.

The raddle is now to be taken apart, and the threads drawn through the slaie, first measuring the slaie by the harness. Begin to draw at the same distance from the end of the slaie, as you suppose it will come out at the other end. The piece is now to be tied on the rod as even as possible, and the treadle cords attached to the harness.

On making a harness, &c.

After the sticks are ready and marked into beers, as a guide to knit on the twine for a harness, you will make the holes for the cords to go through those shafts that are calculated for the top ones, at an equal distance from the ends, say 5 inches from each end for the top shafts, and 6 or 7 inches from the end, for the bottom shafts. These shafts should be made of an exact length before they are marked. The 4 top ones should be all marked across them at once, also the 4 bottom ones. The holes must be made exactly opposite each other, otherwise the harness will not spring true. The cords connected with the two front wings or harness, will now be attached to the front short lamb, (some weavers use short lambs only) and the back wings with the other. The cords attached to these lambs, goes one between the long lambs, and the other outside of them.

Weaving.

It is believed that weavers who are in the practice of making the cloth rough and uneven, do not consider that there is a great difference in the value of two pieces of cloth, of an equal weight and fineness, but differing materially in smoothness and evenness: but we have frequently known this difference to be more than half the price of weaving a yard of cloth.

We shall now point out to the new beginner, a few rules which if strictly attended to, he may be sure of making smooth and even cloth. After the cords belonging to the lambs and those connected with the top of the harness are made even, and of an equal tightness, you will be ready for weaving.

When the treadle is trod down as far as you intend, the instant it is down you must bring the lathe up to the cloth; that is you must have the lathe strike exactly at the time of bringing down the treadle: this you will find will have a good effect to produce a handsome selvage, and smooth, even cloth. Should the above rule not be attended to, especially if the harness is hung low, or the yarn beam too high, it would often cause the upper side of the warp, when the foot is down, to be slack; this would give the thread of filling which you close, a chance of crowding rather on the top of the last one. This is one of the principal causes of cloth being in rows or as many weavers term it, rowey.

There is also another particular reason why cloth is wove uneven, which is by not paying a right attention to striking the lathe after stopping, from changing the bobbin or quill, or other reasons. After changing the bobbin or quill, it is necessary that you strike the lathe once in the last shade, and once in the shade you intend to throw the shuttle through, before you shoot the shuttle again.

When the temples are shifted, they must not be placed nearer than one inch from the yarn, and should be shifted once in about three inches.

When the piece is let down, care should be taken that the lathe should be brought to with that suitable force that will produce the same thickness of cloth, as when it is near the harness.

Observations on wool.

Farmers in taking the wool from the sheep, should be careful to keep the wool together as much as possible, and to avoid cutting the harl or fibres of the wool twice, as the short wool will be wasted.

In putting up the fleece, it will be proper to crowd it in as small a compass as possible; then throw in the edges and roll it up as small as possible without taering. In this way the fleece is kept together, so that in assorting, it will be found easy to the assorter.

Assorting wool.

To perform this work with exactness, it will be proper to attend to the following directions. In the first place prepare two or more boards plained smooth; place them in the form of a bench or table, sufficiently wide to contain the fleece when spread out. When it is fixed in this manner, undo your fleece carefully, first with the outside down, then turn your fleece over and make your choice.

It is well to make 4 sorts, but 3 will answer in many cases. Begin by taking the coarsest first, which you will find at the extremity of the hind quarters of the fleece, being the fourth quality.

In the next place, take off the neck, rump, and belly part for your third quality.

Next take off the shoulders, and a narrow strip down through the back, and so on to the hips and flank part for your second quality, leaving the sides for the finest part or first quality.

In assorting the wool, be careful to keep the different qualities of the wool separate from each other, for should you mix one lock of the coarse wool with the fine, it will be much to the disadvantage of the cloth, particularly as to its beauty: or should you mix fine wool with the coarse, the greatest part of the fine would work out in going through the different operations in manufacturing it into yarn and cloth.

In preparing your wool for different pieces of cloth you must be particular in following these directions.

If you have fine wool sufficient to make a piece of cloth the length you wish, you will then make use of it for warp and filling; but if you have not, then make use of your first quality for the filling, and the second quality of wool for the warp.

By proceeding in this way it will be difficult for the best judges to discover the difference in the quality, and you will easily discover the propriety of the above remarks, by paying attention to a few words that follow.

1st. The quality of cloth is discovered and produced from the filling. In the first place by the quality of the wool.

2d, In spinning—3d, in weaving, napping and finishing.

First, your fine wool should be of the best quality for filling—second, spin your filling as slack as it will bear and follow the shuttle—third, for 20 pounds of warp, use 28 pounds of filling.

In following this last rule, you will find that no greater proportion of weight of filling will finally be left in the body of the cloth than warp, as the finishing and dressing is from the filling.

Cleansing of Wool.

For the purpose of cleansing wool, you must prepare an iron kettle of 40 or 50 gallons, near a stream of water, where you can rinse the wool as soon as it comes out of the kettle.

For factories it will be proper to fix a wooden box 3 or 4 feet square, set in a situation so that a stream of water can run through it, for the use of rinsing the wool when taken from the kettle.

For families a common sized kettle will answer, and a basket for rinsing.

In the first place fill the kettle two thirds full of water and one third of urine, that which is old if you can get it. You will then heat this liquor as warm as you can bear your hand in it for one or 2 seconds without scalding. Then put 5 or 6 pounds of wool loosely into it and keep it turning round for 6 or 8 minutes, or perhaps longer. You may ascertain when it has been in long enough by often squeezing it with your hand, if the grease starts, and the wool appears loose and clear, it has been in a sufficient time.

The wool is then to be taken out upon a board, which must be placed on the edge of the kettle for the purpose of draining it, and saving the liquor. As soon as it is sufficiently drained, rinse the wool until it runs off quite clear. The warmer the wool is, when put in to rinse it the better.

You will then add a second time, 6 or 8 pounds of wool, and proceed as before mentioned; then add some fresh water to the kettle, and continue scouring and rinsing through the day.

Next morning skim off the greasy substance that rises on the top of the liquor, and heat and replenish it by adding 4 or 5 gallons of urine, then fill it up with fresh water.

The liquor when it is 5 or 6 days old is preferable to new: never throw away the liquor, in time of cleansing, unless it should stand for two or three months in the summer without being used.

When the liquor is new, it will be well to put into 40 or 50 gallons, about 6 or 8 ounces of pearlash or potash.

Should the wool not be perfectly clean, as it will not sometimes in full blooded merino wool, you will in that case add ¾ of a pound of fuller's earth, in the first place, and afterwards a little at a time through the day. Dry your wool thoroughly after rinsing, in a clean place, and it is fit for carding.

On Carding of Wool.

It is of the greatest importance that wool should be properly carded, in order to manufacture it right; on this depends the evenness of the yarn, and in some measure the durability of the cloth. If it should not be carded well, it is impossible to make good yarn, and consequently the cloth made from it, will be rather of an inferior quality.

Wool must be in the first place prepared in a proper manner for the machine, in order to produce good rolls. It should be well sorted, and fine wool should be cleansed from all grease: it should then be run through the picker, and spread on the floor for oiling. Take for every 10 pounds of wool one quart of oil, and with a water-pot (such as is used for whitening) or with the hand sprinkle the oil evenly on the wool. Olive oil is to be preferred, as it works the most free. Neats foot is the next best, winter Sperm. oil the next, and summer do. the next.

After it is oiled it should go through the picker again. If it is the finest of wooll, it should be roke or carded twice: the first time of carding it should not be fed on the machine more than one third or fourth as heavy as it would require to make rolls. After this you can proceed to make rolls. Coarse or common wool does not require so much oil as fine—neither does it want breaking, except when worked in mixtures. In making mixtures, particular care must be taken to have the colors well mixed. They should be picked separately, and then a laying of one kind spread upon the floor, near the feeding table of the picker, and the other color or colors, spread even upon the first; so continue spreading one laying on the top of the other, until you have spread the whole. Then take from the top laying down to the floor, as much as you can enclose under one arm, and with the other hand feed it on the picker. After it is picked, oil as before directed; then pick it twice more. After this it should be broke, then picked again: you will then take a small lock, and by working it in your hand with a little soap, will mat it together; by this it will be readily perceived whether it is mixed even or not. If it is mixed even, you will then proceed to make rolls of it; but if not it must be broke again. To find whether rolls are good or not, take up one or more and look through to the light; if well carded they will be perfectly clear, and by stretching them, the harle or fibres will draw out to their full length.

On Spinning Wool.

Spinning is a branch of manufacture, that requires a strict attention, and a steady hand to perform it well. By observing the directions hereafter mentioned, spinners will find it to their advantage.

1st. To spin fine yarn, or that which is 80 knots to the pound, on a common Jenny, with a stretch of six feet, have your ropings as fine as to take up 2 feet 3 or 4 inches of the stretch; then shut in your ropings and begin drawing your thread with as much twist as the thread will bear and not break.

Should you, after taking the twist from the roping, draw your thread with too little twist, it would draw into fine places, and become rough and uneven.

2d. Spinners should use the greatest care in building their copps, or broaches; if they are careless in that particular, the expense of winding and waste of yarn, becomes so great as to take off a considerable share of the profits. To avoid this, begin running the yarn as low down as the spindle will admit. Spread the yarn no wider than one inch, in the first place; you will then keep the copp, or broach, as large as convenient, observing not to run the thread below the largest part, keeping your copps in a proper form, until finished, so that the thread will run from the top end, as from a bobbin. Copps or broaches properly made, are preferred to spools for warping; they are likewise allowed to be better for winding from for bobbins and quills than from skeins or reeled yarn.

Warping of Woollen.

For the purpose of Warping, bars should be preferred, in particular to warp woollen yarn from cops or broaches; a mill in other cases will answer an equal purpose, and by many would be preferred.

To warp a woollen web, 20 spools or cops is a sufficient number for a set. Begin at the top to take your lease, by first making a knot at the ends; run your hand through the division of your spools or cops, quite up to the knot: then place your left hand thumb through this division, drawing the knot close down to the ball of the thumb.

In the next place with your right hand, begin taking the lease at about the distance the pins in the bars are from your left hand. First take the lower thread on the bottom division, being under side of your right hand, and over the thumb: next of the upper division, upper side of your hand and under your thumb, and so on until you have taken up all the threads.

You will now lay up your lease as you have it in the right hand; then draw the lease taken between your right and left hand out to the knot, in the first end of your piece. The next lease you will take in the same way, by saving the lease that is drawn out in the beginning; lay your lease as you hold them in your hand on the pins, excepting the first, which you will lay on the division that is on your thumb over the first pin in going up: then draw your lease and the lower division comes at the top; then carry it straight over to the thumb pin, by bringing the two divisions, one down, and the other up; then turn your right hand up as in the first place, which crosses the divisions between the thrum pins: then lay the upper division over the last pin as you go down, by having the lease right in the lease pins.

Sizing of Woollen,

AS PRACTICED IN THE FACTORIES.

For 20 pounds of woollen warp, dissolve in 12 quarts

of water, $2\frac{1}{2}$ pounds of best Irish glue in a pot or kettle over a moderate fire, by stirring it often to keep it from sticking or burning at the bottom.

When it is dissolved, prepare a tub perfectly smooth, so that your yarn may be kept in good order; then pour off your glue liquor one third part of it into the tub.

Begin at the knot thrumbs of your warped piece, by curling it round in the bottom of your tub and pressing it down at the same time, until you have got one third of the web placed in the tub: now turn the warped piece bottom side up, and be careful that all your yarn is wet, having the glue liquor so warm as not to scald. You will now begin at the end of the web and wring, by taking one hand over the other, until all the first wetting is wrung, which must be taken outside of the tub as fast as it is wrung. Then add a third part of the glue liquor again, and also a third part of the yarn, and proceed as before, until it is all wet and wrung. Observe to wring it no harder than to prevent it from draining.

You will then spread your yarn upon a stretch, out of doors, keeping it from the ground; then run your raith or raddle through it, as you would in beaming; then take out your raith and dry it.

When it is dry, see that your knots or bouts are even, and tie a small string around the web, once in about five yards of each other; then chain it up, and it is ready for beaming.

Beaming the Web.

In order to prepare for this operation, you must have the girth or top beam which is over the seat of your loom made smooth; carry the end of the web over this girth, and bring it down on the yarn beam; then put your rod prepared for that purpose into the lease. You will next place the knots or bouts in the raith or raddle, the width you will have your cloth, by carefully observing that you have the piece equally divided in the width of the loom.

In the next place you will proceed to wind on your piece, keeping the yarn perfectly smooth on the beam, so that there shall be no uneven places or ridges. Should you be careless in that respect, and suffer the bouts to drop into the hollows, the yarn while weaving will part of it become loose, and shew the effect of it in the flannel. As a remedy against this, move your raith moderately backwards and forwards, at different periods in the course of beaming. When it is nearly all wound on, place in your lease rods, and tie the ends together, so that the lease will be safe; then put in a stiff rod through your thrumbs, spread the piece on this rod, and make fast a cord to the rod, to hold the remaining part of the web, and finish beaming.

You will then hang up the raith or raddle nearly over the harness, cut your thrums and bring your lease rods level; then knot up the ends, and it is ready for drawing.

Weaving Woollen.

Weaving is an important part of manufacturing goods. The cloth should be well made by the weaver, otherwise it cannot afterwards be made good. It is a mistaken idea that many people assume, that flannel should be made thin. When flannels are made in this manner, it is impossible for the clothier to give satisfaction, as it lastly devolves on him; he is reproached for some mismanagement, and many times when he is entirely blameless.

Flannels for fulled cloth, should be made as stout as possible by the weaver; at least they should put in of filling one quarter more than warp.

It may be supposed by many that the same quantity of wooll thus wove, will not produce the same proportion or number of yards of cloth when fulled, as if wove thin; but this is a mistake: it should be considered that it requires less fulling than when otherwise done.

It is no doubt noticed by many, that domestic made cloth when worn thread bare, the thread has the appearance of a kink; this is owing to the flannel being wove thin, which requires so much fulling before it arrives at a suitable thickness, that the threads become crooked and knotty.

Should your cloth be wove thick, with the threads brought firm and close one with another, the cloth when worn thread bare, will appear nearly as smooth and handsome as in the first wear of it.

On preparing the filling for Winding.

If you will have a good piece of flannel, wet your bobbins or quills in weak soap suds, and be sure to have your filling thoroughly wet.

To do this in a proper manner, take a small quill or tube, 6 or 8 inches long, and place the tube fairly upon the bobbin or quill, while holding it under the suds liquor, when by sucking the air out the yarn, it will wet with the greatest ease.

Raith or Raddle.

Some attention is necessary to be paid to this instrument, for beaming your piece. For broad weaving, you will have the raith the full width you wish your cloth, whether eleven quarters or under. Calculate the teeth within that distance to take up a web of a middling fineness, by placing every half bout between each of those teeth. In webs, finer or coarser, where you have occasion to place your bouts or half bouts, in double or skipping teeth, be careful to divide the half knots or bouts at such distances, as to give an even proportion, in spreading the yarn on the beam properly.—This utensil being of a simple construction, it will require but a few words to direct how it should be made. In the first place, plane a stick smooth, one and a half inches square. After ascertaining the number of teeth you will want, set them within the distance you want your cloth, by dividing the distance with a pair of compasses or dividers, having them the size of a quill, and 2½ or 3 inches in length; then frame in a couple of posts at each end, with tenons for a cap piece, which last must be grooved out to set on the ends of the teeth, having small pins to keep it to its place, and it is finished.

Weaving Draft.

Before we commence giving directions, as it respects the various drafts which follow, it will be proper to give some explanation of terms, that are used; which will answer for a guide in many respects for all the drafts in our work, if strict attention is paid to the subject.

A short cord, is a cord fixed to the long lam and treadle; this cord raises up a wing or shaft of the harness, when the weaver treads the treadle, to which it is attached.

A long cord, is a cord that is fixed to the short lam, and passes between the long lams, and connects with the treadle: when this treadle is trod, it pulls down a part of the wings of the harness.

Wings of the harness, are a number of shafts, on which are worked a kind of loop with twine; through these, the warp passes. The wings are connected with the jacks above, and short lams below, by the help of cords.

Long lam, is a long stick which is raised up and down while weaving, by being connected with the treadle, by the help of a short cord. The long lams raise up the wings when the treadles are trod down by means of the short cords, and other cords which follow from the ends of the long lams to the ends of the jacks on the top of the loom. These jacks are a number of sticks which move on a pin in a frame at the top of the loom.

Short lam, is similar to a long lam only shorter, and moves on another pin above the long lams. The short lams pull down the wings when the treadle is trod by help of the long cords; they should be placed in the loom so far above the long lams as not to touch them when the treadle is firmly down.

Draft, is a form of directions by which to commence and perform work in weaving. Also in drawing through the warp into the harness, it is termed the draft.

Cording, is a name found in all of the above drafts. and made to distinguish the long and short cords. The long cords are distinguished by crosses, and the short cords by blank spaces.

N. B. The learner will see that the long lams cannot be represented in any of the drafts, excepting in those that are not connected with the cording: as for instance they are not seen in draft No. 1, but are in No. 17. The short lams are not to be seen in any of the drafts: we therefore refer the reader to the engraving, which shews the treadles, lams, wings &c.

The front wing of the harness in the following numbers of drafts, will have knit on it double the number of helves that each of the other wings have: and when drawing, there will be left out opposite the figures one helve to two threads drawn: viz, in numbers, 8, 9, 10, 12, 13 14, 16, 18, 19, 22, 23, 25, and 28.

No. I. Bird Eyes.

DRAFT.

After the cords of the harness are made even, so that they will hang level; you will then commence drawing on the right. Begin on the back wing, and draw A, B, C, & D, then leave out one helve on the front shaft D, next draw C, B, A, and the draft is once over, which is 7 threads. You will then begin again on A, and go over again as before, being careful to put one helve on D. So proceed backwards and forwards until all the the yarn is drawn through the harness.

In the cording there are eight long cords and eight short ones.

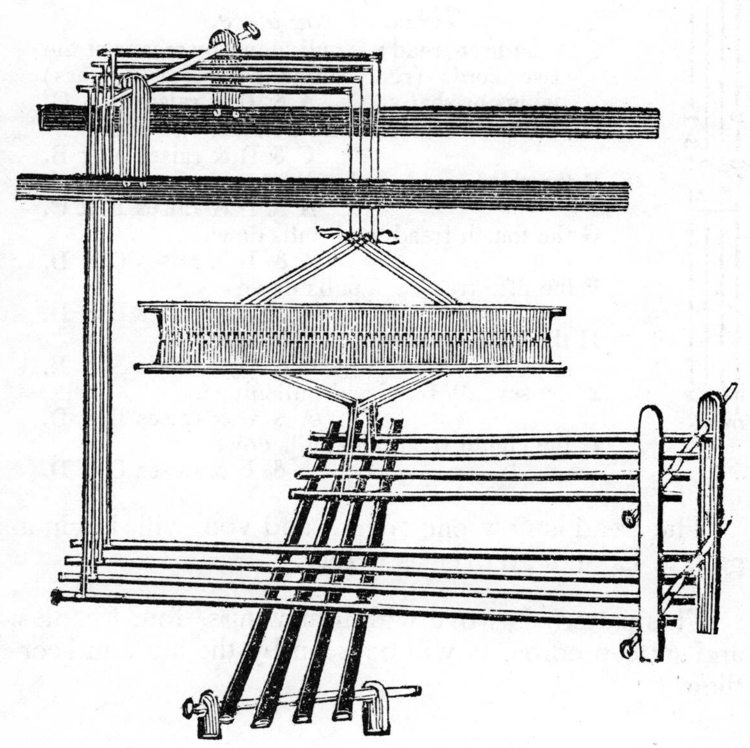

G

No. 1. Bird Eyes.

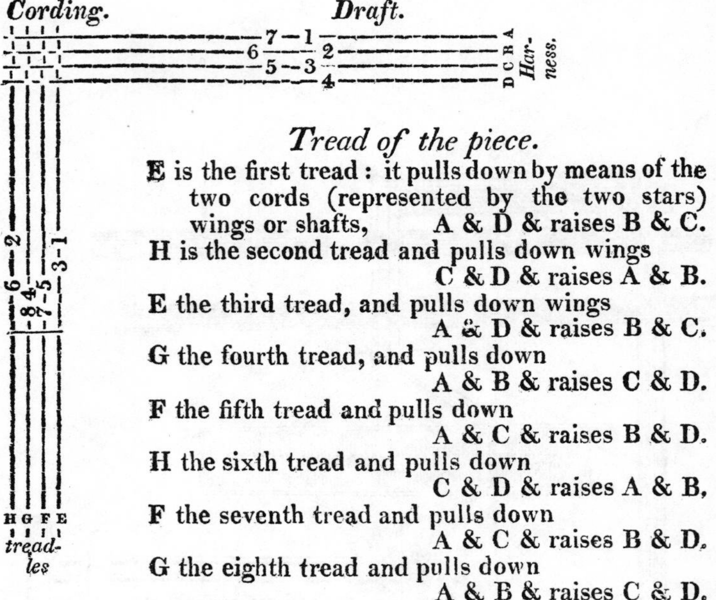

Tread of the piece.

E is the first tread: it pulls down by means of the two cords (represented by the two stars) wings or shafts, A & D & raises B & C.
H is the second tread and pulls down wings C & D & raises A & B.
E the third tread, and pulls down wings A & D & raises B & C.
G the fourth tread, and pulls down A & B & raises C & D.
F the fifth tread and pulls down A & C & raises B & D.
H the sixth tread and pulls down C & D & raises A & B,
F the seventh tread and pulls down A & C & raises B & D.
G the eighth tread and pulls down A & B & raises C & D.

The tread is now once over, and you will begin again at E, and go over as before.

This pattern is wove with four wings, four treadles, and sixteen cords, as will be seen by the draft and cording.

No. 2. Three Shaft Ticking.

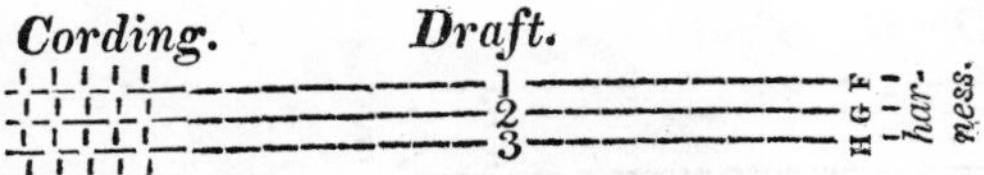

Cording. *Draft.*

1 2 3 — H G F harness.

6 4 5 2 3 1

E D C B A *treadles.*

This pattern is wove with 3 wings, 5 treadles and 15 cords; and the draft is represented as being once drawn over: you will next begin to draw through the back wing F, then the middle one G, then the front one H, and so go over with it in that way until all your yarn is drawn through the harness. The learner will observe that by treading thus, A, C, B, D, C, E, the draft will be twice over, and the treading once. Use the same slaie as for plain cloth, and draw 3 threads through a reed or split.

No. 3. Four Shaft Ticking.

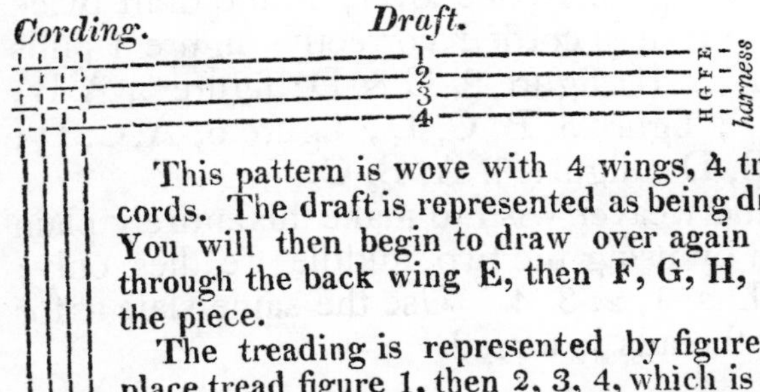

Cording. *Draft.*

1 2 3 4 — H G F E *harness*

2 4 3 1

Treadles

This pattern is wove with 4 wings, 4 treadles, and 16 cords. The draft is represented as being drawn over once. You will then begin to draw over again as before, first through the back wing E, then F, G, H, and so through the piece.

The treading is represented by figures. In the first place tread figure 1, then 2, 3, 4, which is once over; then begin again as before and tread figure 1, and so on. Use a slaie two beers lower than for plain cloth, and draw 4 threads in a reed.

No. 4. Elastic Cord.

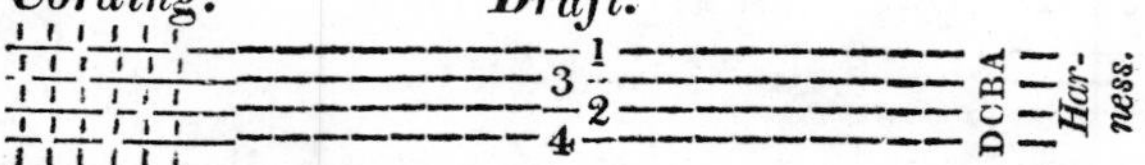

Cording. *Draft.*

1 3 2 4 D C B A *Harness.*

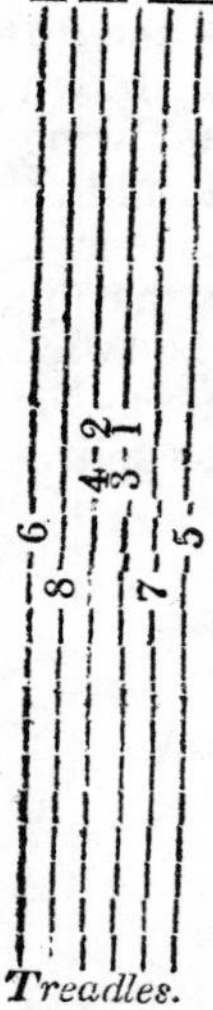

Treadles. 6 8 4 2 3 1 7 5

This pattern is formed by four wings, six treadles and sixteen long cords, which are represented by crosses; these cords connect the short lams and treadles. Eight short cords.—These are represented by the spaces in the cording: they connect the long lams and treadles. See No. 1. Bird eye.

The present draft as it appears, is once drawn over: thus, first drawn thread through wing A, next C, B, D, begin again at A, and so go on as before.

TREAD.

Tread first, figure 1; next, 2, 3, 4, 5, 6, 7, 8. In treading this once over, is the draft twice over. If it is corded correctly, figure 1 pulls down wings A & B; figure 2, C & D; figure 3, A B; figure 4, C, D; figure 5, B, C, D; figure 6, A, C, D; figure 7, A, B, D; figure 8, A, B, C.

Should the weaver wish to make this entirely plain cloth, he can by using the two middle treadles only; as directed; thus, 1, 2, 3, 4. Use the same slaie as for plain cloth, 2 threads in a reed.

No. 5. Herring Bone.

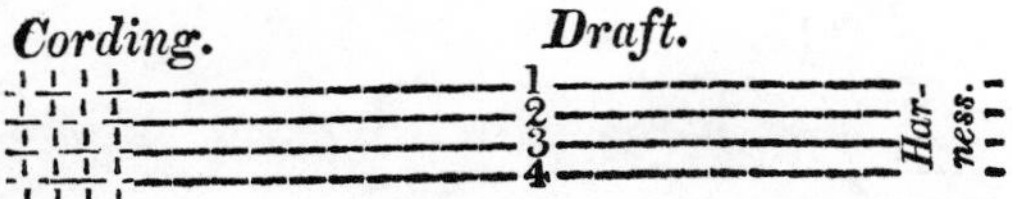

Cording. *Draft.*

Harness.

The figures on this draft represent it as being drawn once over; you will then begin again at figure 1, and go over in the same manner. There is in the cording to this draft, 8 cords that are represented by crosses, and also 8 that are represented by spaces. The eight that are distinguished by crosses, are long cords that connect the short lams and treadles. The spaces, are cords connecting the long lams and treadles.

Treadles

TREAD.

If the cording is correct, the treadles will pull down the wings as follows: First tread pulls down wings, figures 1 & 2; second, figures 2 & 3; third, figures 3 & 4; fourth, 1 & 4: fifth, 3 & 4; sixth, 2 & 3; seventh, 1 & 2; eighth, 1 & 4.

The tread is now once over, and the draft twice.—Use a slaie 4 beers finer than for plain cloth, and draw 2 threads in a reed.

No. 6. Six Shaft Twill.

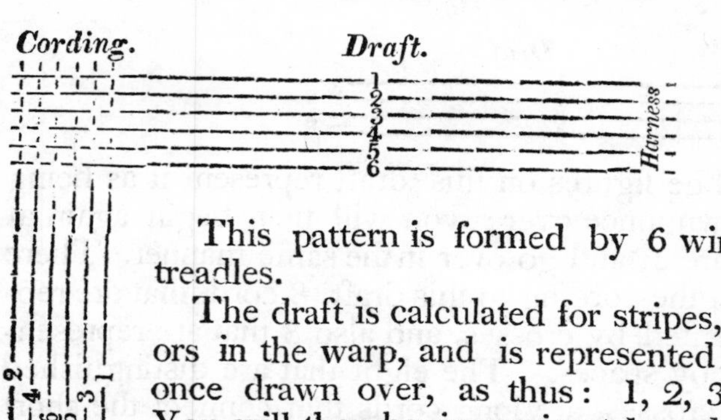

This pattern is formed by 6 wings and 6 treadles.

The draft is calculated for stripes, two colors in the warp, and is represented as being once drawn over, as thus: 1, 2, 3, 4, 5, 6. You will then begin again at 1, and go on as before.

In this cording there are 18 crosses, or long cords, attached to the short lams and treadles, and 18 spaces, or short cords, which are attached to long lams and treadles.

If the cording is correct, figure 1 on the treadles, which is the first tread, pulls down fig. 4, 5 & 6, on the harness; figure 2 pulls down 1, 5 & 6; figure 3, pulls down 1, 2 & 6; figure 4, pulls down 1, 2 & 3; figure 5, pulls down 2, 3 & 4; figure 6, 3 4 & 5.

You will use a slaie six beers finer than for plain cloth, and draw 2 threads in a reed.

No. 7. Bird Eyes & Twilled.

Cording. *Draft.*

Harness. A B C D E F G H

Treadles,

This pattern is formed with 8 wings in the harness, and six treadles. The draft is represented as being drawn once over, viz: draw first on E, then F, G, H, then the back wing A, then on C, B, C, A, D, B, D. On the 4 back wings, the learner will perceive we skip shafts. You will now begin again, on E, and so on, according to the figures on the shafts of the harness; observing that in drawing the pattern once over, will take 32 threads. The cording is represented by 12 crosses, and 36 spaces. The crosses or long cords being attached to the short lams, will pull down a part of the wings, while the spaces or short cords attached to the long lams, raise the rest of the wings.

TREAD.

Begin first on treadle figure 1, which pulls down wings D, and E.

next on figure 2, pulls down A and F.
fig. 3, pulls down C and G.
fig. 4, pulls down A and H.
fig. 5, pulls down D and E.
fig. 6, pulls down B and F.
fig. 7, pulls down C and G.
fig. 8, pulls down B and H.

The treading of the pattern is now once over: begin again on fig. 1, and go on as before. The pattern of the cloth is formed of 2 colors in the warp, drawn 8 and 8. For the filling you will use a different color. The bird's eye appears in the filling, and the twill in the warp. Use a slaie 4 beers finer than for plain cloth, and draw 2 threads in a reed. The warp and filling are to be of an equal fineness.

No. 8. Figured Chambray.

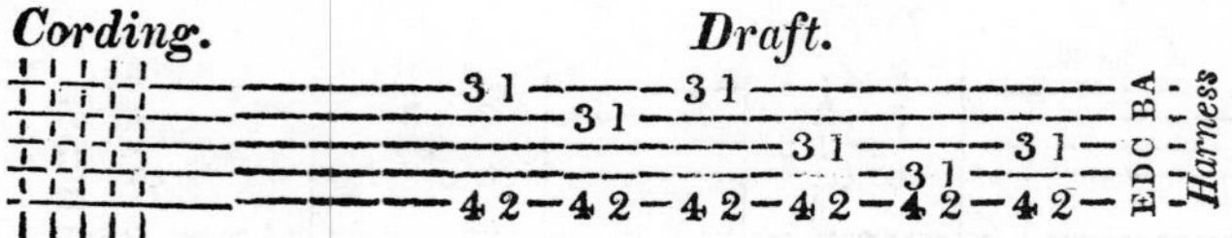

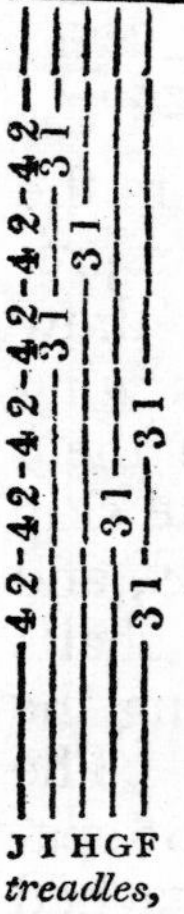

Cording. *Draft.*

```
--------31---31-------------- A
-----------31---------------- B
-----------------31------31-- C
---------------------31------ D
--------42-42-42-42-42-42---- E
                        Harness
```

```
42-42-42-42-42-42   J
31-31               I
31                  H
31-31               G
31-31               F
```

J I H G F *treadles,*

This pattern is formed with 5 wings and 5 treadles. The draft is represented as being once drawn over, viz: draw first on C, next on E, C, E, D, E, D, E, and so on through, there being 24 threads drawn. You will then begin again on C, as at first.

The cording is represented by 12 crosses, and 13 spaces, the crosses represent the long cords that connect the short lams and treadles, and the spaces, the short cords that connect the long lams and treadles.

TREAD.

Begin first on treadle I, next on J, I, J, H, J, H, J, and so on through, as the treadle draft directs; the left foot when weaving being continued on treadle J.

Use a slaie 2 beers finer than for plain cloth and draw 2 threads in a reed.

No. 9. Diamonds & Squares for Diaper.

Cording. *Draft.*

```
------------------------------3 1-------------------------  A
--------------------3 1-----------3 1---------------------  B
-------------3 1---------------------------3 1------------  C
------3 1---------------------------------------3 1-------  D
--------------------------------------------------------3 1  E
------4 2-4 2-4 2-4 2-4 2-4 2-4 2-4 2-4 2---------------------  F
                                                    Harness.
```

This pattern is formed with 6 treadles and 6 wings in the harness, observing that half of the threads are drawn on the front wing F. The draft represents the threads being drawn once over. It begins thus: first drawn thread on E, which is the second wing from the front; next drawn is F, then again E, F, then D, F, D, F, C, F, C, F, B, F, B, F, A, F, A, F, B, F, B, F, C, F, C, F, D, F, D, F. You will then begin to draw again as before, on E. F, observing that you will draw 32 threads, to form the draft once over.

The cording is represented by 15 crosses, and 21 spaces. The crosses are shewn for long cords, to be attached to the short lams, and will pull down a part of the wings. The spaces represent short cords, attached to long lams, which raise the rest of the wings.

GH.IJKL. *treadles*,

TREAD.

In the treading, you will observe to begin the tread on treadle I, then G, I, G, J, G, J, G, K, G, K, G, L, G, L, G, and so on, until the tread is through; next begin at the top of the column as before, observing that it takes 32 treads to form the figure, and that the left foot while weaving this figure is always on treadle G, which makes the plain part of the cloth, while the rest of the treadles make the flower. Use a slaie 2 beers finer than for plain cloth, and draw 2 threads in a reed. The figure is a diamond of 16 blocks.

No. 10. Diamond Diaper.

Cording. *Draft.*

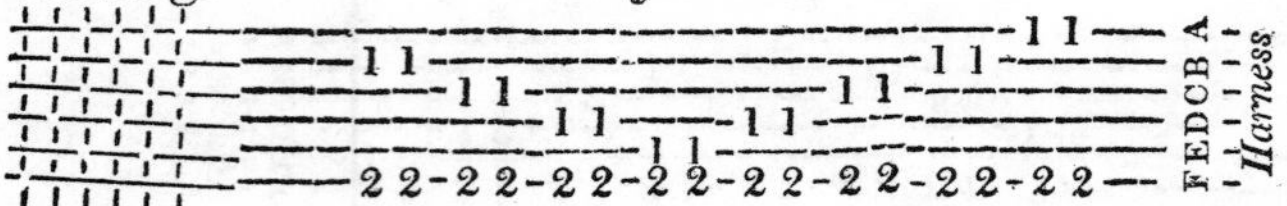

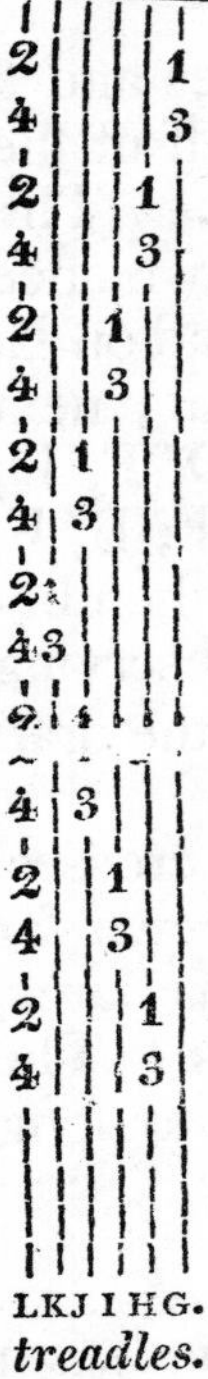

```
A ---------------------------------------------11------
B ------11------------------------------11-------------
C ----------11--------------------11-------------------
D --------------11----------11-------------------------
E ------------------11---------------------------------
F ------22-22-22-22-22-22-22-22------------------------
```

FEDCBA *Harness.*

LKJIHG. *treadles.*

This pattern is formed with 6 wings and 6 treadles—observing that half of the threads are drawn on the front wing, F. The draft is represented as being once drawn over. First begin to draw at figure 1, on the back wing A, next on the front wing F, then again on A, next on F, and so on from figure 1 to figure 2, as you will find pointed out on the 6 wings of the harness, until you get the figure in the draft all drawn: then begin again as before to draw on A, and F, taking notice that you will draw 32 threads to form the figure once over, which is when wove, a diamond of 25 blocks.

The cording is represented by 19 crosses, which signify long cords to be attached to the short lams, also by 17 spaces, which signify short cords, which are attached to long lams.

TREAD.

The treading is represented by figures, and is directed at the top of the treadle draft how to begin the tread, which is thus,—Fig. 1, which is treadle G, figure 2, is treadle L, and so on until you tread the figure through, and you will find it takes 32 treads to form it, and that the left foot while weaving, is always on the left treadle L, which makes the plain part of the cloth, while the rest make the flower. If instead of the above figure you wish a diamond of 9 blocks only, you will begin the tread on treadle I, and tread through all the treadles to the left, then back as far as treadle J. Use a slaie 4 beers finer than for plain cloth, and draw 2 threads in a reed.

No. 11. Bags, (wove whole.)

This pattern is formed with 8 treadles and six wings. Draw the first thread on the back wing, figure 1, next on 2, 3, 4, 5, 6, and it is drawn once over; then begin again on the back wing and go through as before, and so on until all the threads are drawn.

In the cording there is 24 long cords, on short lams, and 24 short cords on long lams.

TREAD.

First begin to tread figure 1, next figures 2, 3, 4, 5, 6. These treadles form the body of the bag. The tread is to be continued over and over in that way, until the bag is wove as long as you wish: you will then tread the two outside treadles A and B, which will close up the end of the bag.

The right foot on treadle figure 1, takes down 5 wings and raises up one: the left foot fig. 2, takes down one wing and raises up five, and operates in that manner through the tread.

Linen yarn for a 30 slaie, will be suitable for this pattern, and draw 6 threads in a reed.

No. 12. Diamond of 9 Blocks...Diaper.

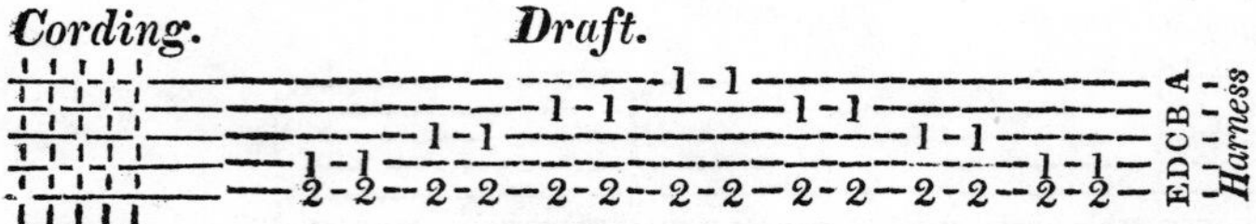

Cording. *Draft.*

```
----------------------------1-1-------------------------------- A
-----------------------1-1---------1-1------------------------- B
------------1-1--------------------------1-1------------------- C
--1-1-------------------------------------------1-1------------ D
--2-2--2-2--2-2--2-2--2-2--2-2--2-2--2-2--2-2------------------ E
                                                           Harness
```

```
2   1
4   3
2  1
4  3
2 1
4 3
21
43
2 1
4 3
2  1
4  3
2   1
4   3
JIHGF
treadles.
```

This pattern is formed with 5 treadles and 5 wings, and you will notice that half of the threads are drawn on the front wing E. The first thread is drawn on wing D, next E, then on D, E, C, E, C, E, B, E, B, E, A, E, A, E, so continue until through, as the draft represents. Now go over again as before, beginning on D, until the yarn is all drawn through the harness.

In the cording are 13 long cords on the short lams, and 12 short cords on the long lams.

TREAD.

The first tread is on treadle F, fig. 1, on the top of the treadle draft; next fig. 2, treadle J, next F, J, G, J, G, J, H, J, H, J, I, J, I, J, and so on until the draft is trod once over: then begin on F, as before. Treadles F, and J, form the plain cloth, and G, H, I, the flower. If you wish to make it all plain, tread F, and J, constantly.

Use a slaie 2 beers finer than for plain cloth, and draw 2 threads in a reed.

While you are weaving, the left foot is always on treadle J.

No, 13. Rose and Diamond Diaper.

Cording. *Draft.*

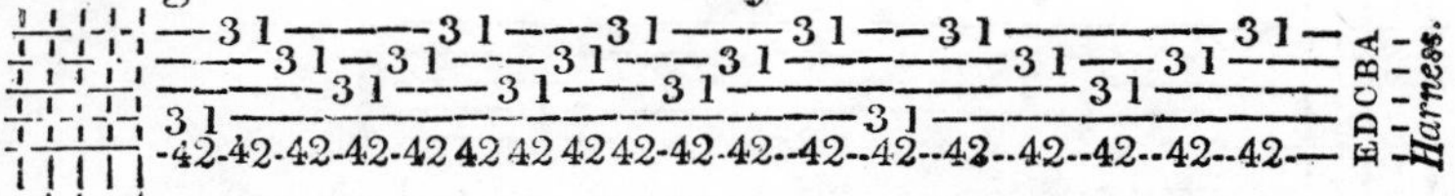

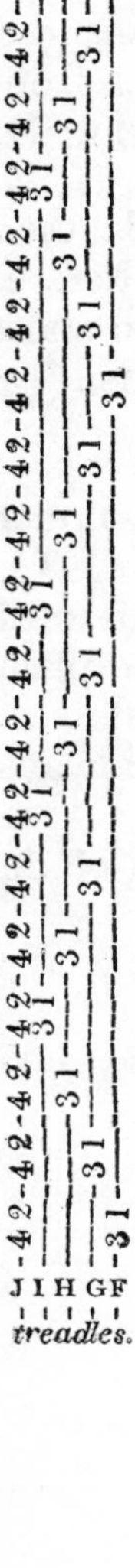

```
—31———31——31———31——31—————31—  A
——31—31——31———31——————31——31———  B
————31———31———31——————————31—————  C
31————————————————31———————————  D
-42-42-42-42-42 42 42 42 42-42-42--42--42--42--42--42--42--42—  E
```
Harness.

This pattern is formed with 5 treadles and 5 wings. Half of the threads are drawn on the front wing E. The first thread is drawn on wing A, next on E, A, E, B, E, B, E, C, E, C, E, and so on until through the whole, as the draft directs; then go over again, beginning on A, as before.

In the cording, there are 13 long cords on the short lams, and 12 short cords on the long lams.

TREAD.

The first tread is on treadle G, figure 1, under the cording; next on J, fig. 2, then on G, J, H, J, H, J, I, J, I, J, and so on until the tread is completed, as directed on the treadle draft. F, and J, form the plain part of the cloth, G, H, and I, form the flower; tread F, and J, constantly, and it will make it all plain.

Use a slaie for this draft, 4 beers finer than for plain cloth, and draw 2 threads in a reed.—While you are weaving, the left foot is always on treadle J.

J I H G F
treadles.

No 14, Eight Block Diamond for Diaper.

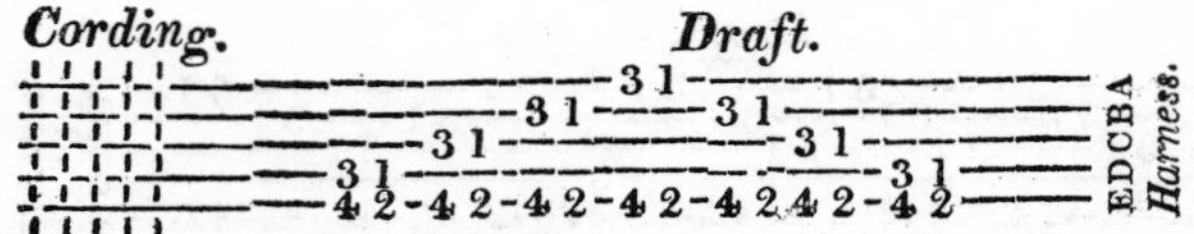

Cording. *Draft.*

```
------------------------31--------------------------- E
-------------------31------31------------------------ D
--------------31-------------------31---------------- C
---------31-----------------------------31----------- B
---------42-42-42-42-42 42 42-42--------------------- A
                                                Harness.
```

```
2   1
4   3
2  1
4  3
2 1
4 3
21
43
2 1
4 3
2  1
4  3
2   1
4   3
J I H G F
Treadles
```

This pattern is formed with 5 treadles and 5 wings. Half of the threads, are drawn on front wing E. The first thread is drawn on wing D, next on E, D, E, C, E, C, E, B, E, B, E, A, E, A, E, so on through the draft, as directed: then draw over again, beginning on D, as before. In the cording there are 12 long Cords on short lams, and 13 short Cords on the long lams.

TREAD.

The first tread is on treadle F, fig. 1, under the cording: next on J, fig. 2; next on F, J, G, J, G, J, H, J, H, J, I, J, I, J, and so on until the tread is completed. F and J, form the plain part of the cloth; G, H, I, form the flower. While you are weaving, the left foot is always on treadle J.

Use a slaie 2 beers finer than for plain cloth, and draw 2 threads in a reed.

No. 15, Cross and Diamond Diaper.

Cording. *Draft.*

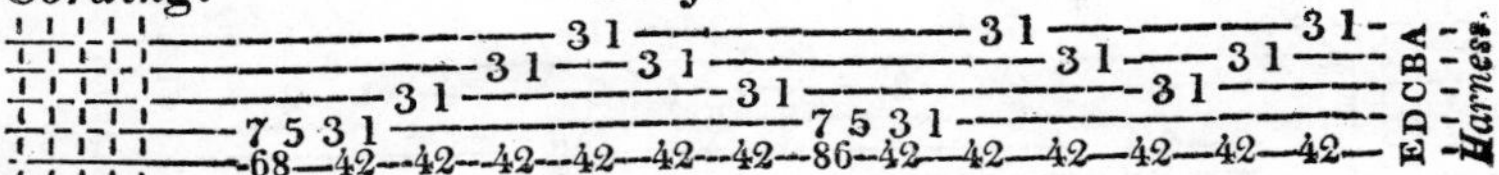

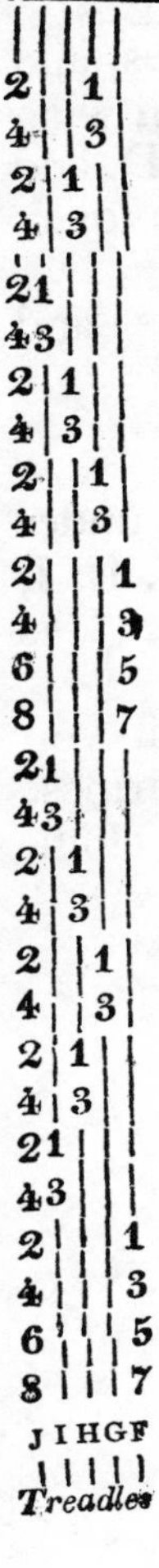

```
                          31                31          31-  A
                   31——31      31                31——31      B
            31                    31                 31      C
  7531                              7531                     D
-68—42—42—42—42—42—42—86—42—42—42—42—42—42—                  E
                                                     EDCBA Harness.
```

```
2 1
4 3
2 1
4 3
21
43
2 1
4 3
2 1
4 3
2 1
4 3
6 5
8 7
21
43
2 1
4 3
2 1
4 3
2 1
4 3
21
43
2 1
4 3
6 5
8 7
JIHGF
Treadles
```

This pattern is formed with 5 treadles, and 5 wings. Half of the threads, are drawn on the front wing E. The first thread is drawn on A, next on E, next on A, E, B, E, B, E,C, E, C, E, and so on through the whole: then begins the second time on A, as before.

There are 12 long cords on short lams, and 13 short cords on the long lams.

TREAD.

The first tread is on treadle G, fig. 1, next on J, fig. 2, next on G, J, H, J, H, J, I, J, I, J, and so on, until the tread is completed.

F and J, form the plain part of the cloth, and G, H, I, the flower. While you are weaving, the left foot is always on treadle J.

Use a slaie 2 beers finer than for plain cloth, and draw 2 threads in a reed.

No, 16, Checked Dimety.

Cording. *Draft.* *Harness.* *Treadles.*

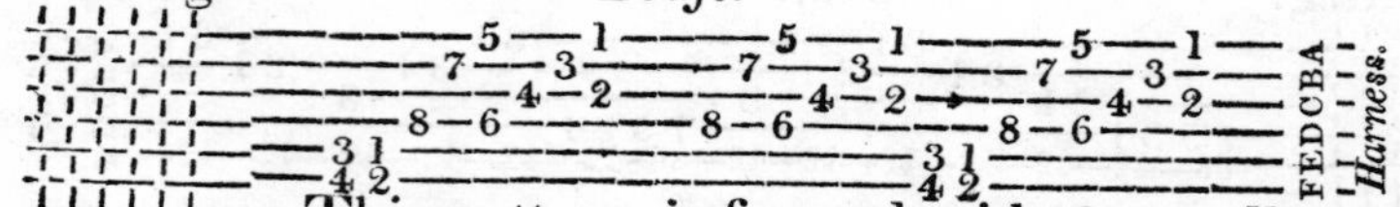

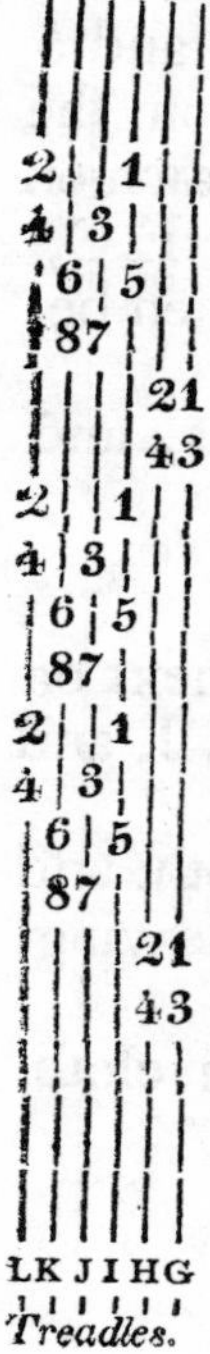

This pattern is formed with 6 treadles, and 6 wings. The first thread, is drawn on wing A, next on C, next on B, C, A, D, B, D, and so on as the draft directs; until once over, then commence again on A, as before.

There are 10 long cords, on short lams: and 26 short cords on long lams.

TREAD.

The first tread, is on treadle I, fig. 1, under the cording, next on L, fig. 2, next on J, L, I, K, J, K, and so on, until the whole tread is completed.

G and H, forms the plain bar, but if you tread I, J, K, L, only, it will form it into stripes.

Use a slaie 2 beers finer than for plain cloth, and draw 2 threads in a reed.

No. 17, Eight Shaft Coverlet.

Draft.

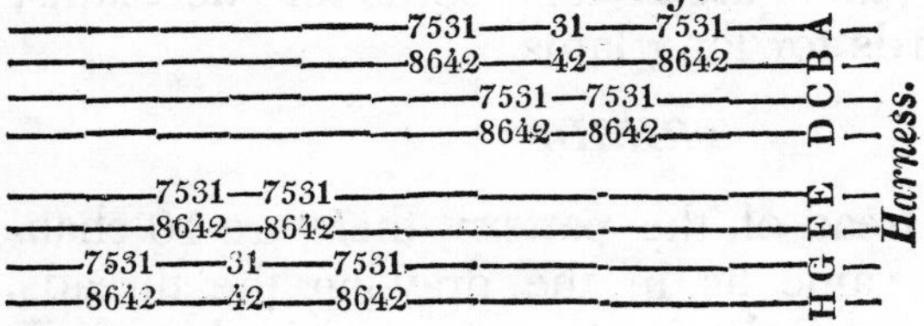

```
——————————————7531——31——7531——A—
——————————————8642——42——8642——B—
————————————————7531—7531—————C—
————————————————8642—8642—————D—

————7531—7531—————————————————E—
————8642—8642—————————————————F—
——7531——31——7531——————————————G—
——8642——42——8642——————————————H—
```

Harness.

Cording. *Lambs.*

ABCDEF

```
1  2
3  4
5  6
7  8
1  2
3  4
5  6
7  8
1  2
3  4
5  6
7  8
1  2
3  4
5  6
7  8
1  2
3  4
5  6
7  8
```

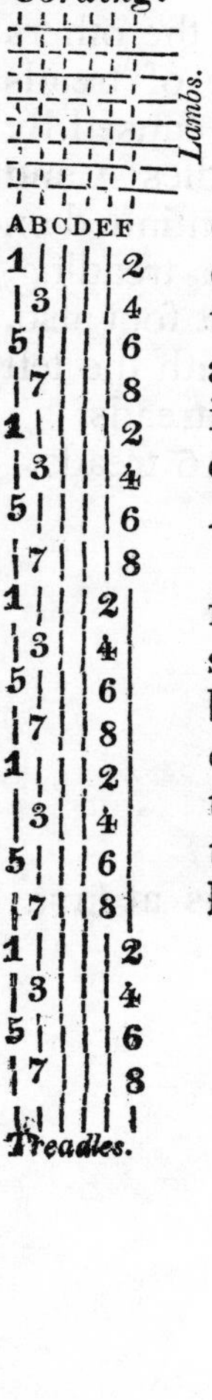

Treadles.

This pattern is formed with 6 treadles, and 8 wings. The wings are represented, as being in two divisions, with 4 wings in each.

You will now begin to draw the first thread, on the back division, wing A, fig. 1, next draw on B, fig. 2, next A, B, A, B, A, B, then on C, D, C, D, C, D, C, D, and so on, as directed through the draft: observing, that it takes 72 threads, to draw the figure once over: you will then begin on the back wing A, as first directed.

Should the weaver wish to have a larger figure, for the coverlet than the draft represents: he may vary it according to his fancy, by observing that the tread is guided by the draft: and that the number of treads in the treadle draft, must be twice the number of threads, that are in the drawing through the harness.

Explanation of Cording and Tread for No. 17.

In the cording, there are 25 long cords for short lams, and 23 short cords for long lams.

TREAD.

In the whole tread of the pattern, there are 10 changes, being the same as in the drawing the threads. There are only three changes represented in the treadle draft for want of room; these three, and all the others described hereafter, have double the number of treads that there are threads in the drawing; this is caused by the binding yarn, which is operated by treadles A and B. You will observe, that the left foot is continued on treadle A and B, through the whole draft in treading, which is 72 treads and 72 treads for the right foot also.

First begin to tread on treadle A, fig. 1, with the left foot, next F, right foot; and so on being 16 treads.

Next right foot on E, (left foot as before) 16 treads.

Right foot on F, 8 treads.
" " on E, 16 treads.
" " on F. 16 treads.
" " on C, 16 treads.
" " on D, 16 treads.
" " on C, 8 treads.
" " on D, 16 treads.
" " on C, 16 treads.

The draft is now once over, begin again as at first.

No. 18, Compass Diaper.

Draft.

```
———31—————31———————————————————————A—
———31—31————31—31——————————————————B—   Hanness.
—————31—31————31—31—31—31—31—31————C—
——————31————————31—31—31—31—31—————D—
———4242424242424242-424242-42424242-4242424242———E—
```

Cording.

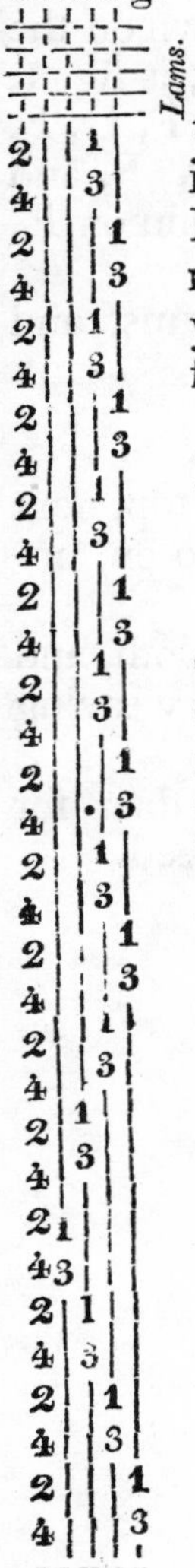

```
        Lams.
2 | | 1 |
4 | 3 |
2 | | 1
4 | | 3
2 | 1 |
4 | 3 |
2 | | 1
4 | | 3
2 | 1 |
4 | 3 |
2 | | 1
4 | | 3
2 | 1 |
4 | 3 |
2 | | 1
4 | • 3
2 | 1 |
4 | 3 |
2 | | | 1
4 | | | 3
2 | | 1 |
4 | | 3 |
2 | 1 | |
4 | 3 | |
2 1 | | |
4 3 | | |
2 | 1 | |
4 | 3 | |
2 | | 1 |
4 | | 3 |
2 | | | 1
4 | | | 3
J I H G F
```

This Pattern is formed with 5 treadles, and 5 wings. Half of the threads, are drawn on the front wing E. The first thread drawn, is fig. 1, on wing C, next on E, then on C, E, D, E, D, E, and so through, as the draft directs. When through, the draft is once over: you will then begin again on wing C, as before.

There are 12 long cords, on short lams, and 13 short cords, on long lams.

TREAD.

The first tread is on treadle G, fig. 1, under the cording, next on treadle J, fig. 2, next on G, J, F, J, F, J, and so on, as far as is represented on the draft. Then continue on with the right foot 4 changes thus, (left foot as before) C 4 treads (including the left foot) H, 4, I, 4, H, 4, which completes the tread.

J, forms the plain part of the cloth, the rest make the flower.

While you are weaving, the left foot is always on treadle J. The slaie should be 2 beers finer than for plain cloth, and drawn 2 threads in a reed.

No. 19, Half Diamond Diaper.

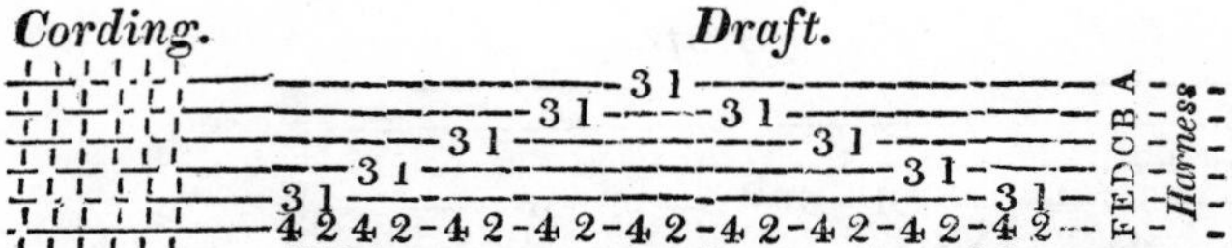

Cording. *Draft.*

```
-------------------------31-----------------------A
------------------31------31--------------------B
-----------31--------------------31-----------C
-----31--------------------------------31-----D
31----------------------------------------31--E
4242-42-42-42-42-42-42-42-42--F
```

Harness

21					
43					
2	1				
4	3				
2		1			
4		3			
2			1		
4			3		
2				1	
4				3	
L	K	J	I	H	G

Treadles.

This pattern is formed with 6 treadles, and 6 wings. Half of the threads are drawn on the front wing F. The first thread drawn, is fig. 1, on wing E, next fig. 2, on F, next E, F, D, F, D, F, C, F, C, F, B, F, B, F, A, F, A, F, and so on through the draft, then begin again on E, as before.

There are 17 long cords on short lams, and 19 short cords on long lams.

TREAD.

The first tread is on K fig. 1, at the top, next on L, next on K, L, J, L, J, L, and so on, until through, as directed.

G and L, form the plain part of the cloth, and the rest the flower. While you are weaving the left foot is always on treadle L.

The slaie should be 2 beers finer than for plain cloth, and drawn 2 threads in a reed.

No. 20, Diamond Coverlet.

This pattern is formed with 6 treadles, and 8 wings. The wings of the harness, are represented as being in two divisions, with four in each.

Draw the first thread, on the front division wing G, fig. 1, next on H, fig. 2, and so on, drawing 8 threads on G and H.

You will next draw

4 threads	on wings	E and F,
4	on	C and D,
4	on	A and B,
4	on	E and F,
4	on	C and D,
4	on	A and B,

and so on, through as the draft directs, being in the whole figure, 104 threads. You will then begin on wing G, as at first.

No. 20· Cording aud Tread.

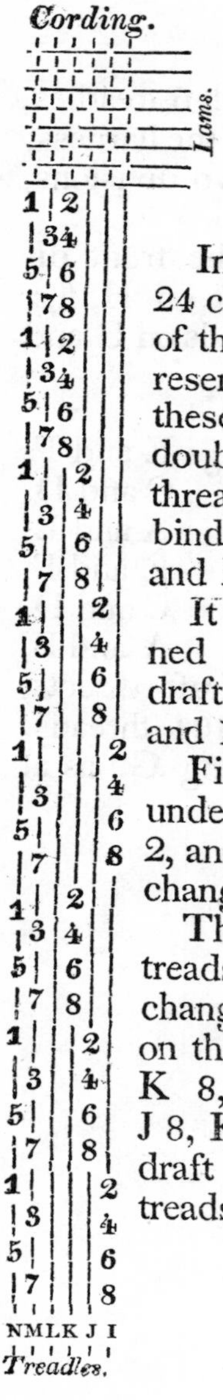

Cording.

Lams.

In the cording there are 25 long cords for short lams, and 23 short cords for long lams.

TREAD.

In the whole tread of the pattern, there are 24 changes, being the same as in the drawing of the threads. There are only 7 changes represented in the treadle draft, for want of room: these 7, as also the rest of the changes, have double the number of treads, that there are threads in the drawing: this is caused by the binding yarn which is trod by treadles N, and M.

It will be observed that the left foot is confined on treadles N and M, through the whole draft of the treading, which is 104 treads; and 104 treads for the right foot also.

First begin the tread, on treadle N, fig. 1, under the cording; next right foot on L, fig. 2, and so on for 16 treads, which is called one change.

The next, right foot on K, 8 treads J, 8 treads I 8, K 8, J 8, I 8, this makes all the changes and treads, that we have represented on the treadles. Then continue on J 8 treads, K 8, I 8, J 8, K 8, L 16, I 8, J 8, K 8, I 8, J 8, K 8, J 8, I 8, K 8, J 8, I 8, the whole draft or figure, is now through, being 208 treads.

N M L K J I

Treadles.

No. 21, Diamond Coverlet.

Draft.

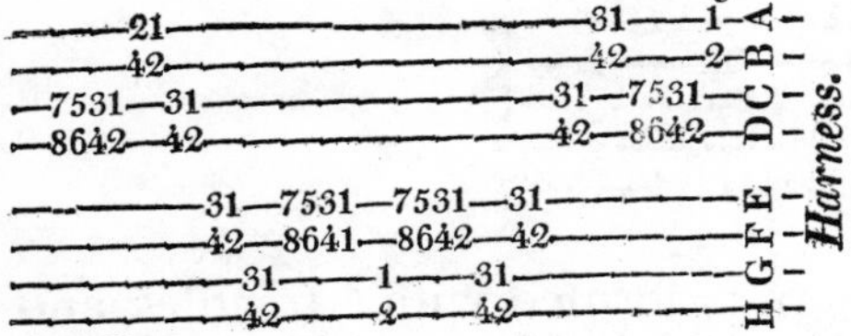

```
——21——————————————31——1—A —
——42——————————————42——2—B —
—7531—31——————————31—7531—C —
—8642—42——————————42—8642—D —   Harness.

————31—7531—7531—31————————E —
————42—8641—8642—42————————F —
————31———1———31————————————G —
————42———2———42————————————H —
```

Cording.

Lams.

```
1 2
3 4
1 2
3 4
5 6
7 8
1 2
3 4
5 6
7 8
1 2
3 4
5 6
7 8
1 2
3 4
5 6
7 8
1 2
3 4
5 6
7 8
1 2
3 4
5 6
7 8
NMLK JI
```

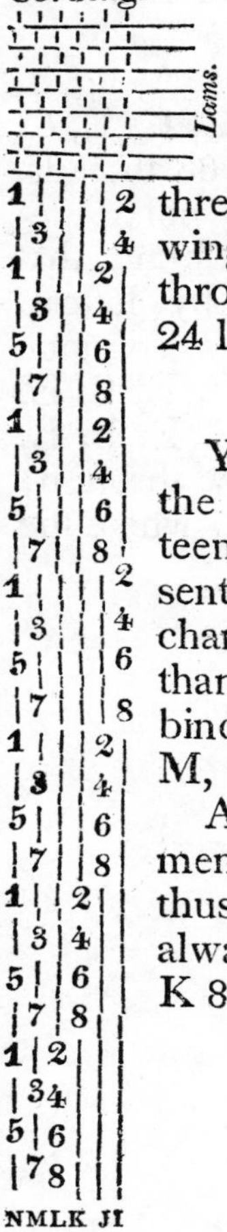

Treadles.

This pattern has 6 treadles, and 8 wings, the last are seen in the two divisions.

Draw the first thread on the back wing A, fig. 1, next B, fig. 2, next draw 8 threads on wings C and D, next 4 threads on wings A, B, then draw 4 on C, D, and so on through the draft as directed, being 68 threads. 24 long cords, and 24 short cords.

TREAD.

You will tread thus, first on N, fig. 1, under the cording, next on I, fig. 2, and so on fourteen changes, although there are but six represented on the treadles, for want of room. These changes have double the number of treads, than the threads in the drawing, caused by the binding yarn, which is trod by treadles N and M, with the left foot.

After treading the six changes as abovementioned, you will go on and tread 8 more thus, right foot on K, 16 treads, (the left foot always on N and M,) L, 4 treads, K 16, L 8, K 8, J 8, I 8, J 16, and the tread is once over.

No. 22, Diamond Diaper.

Draft.

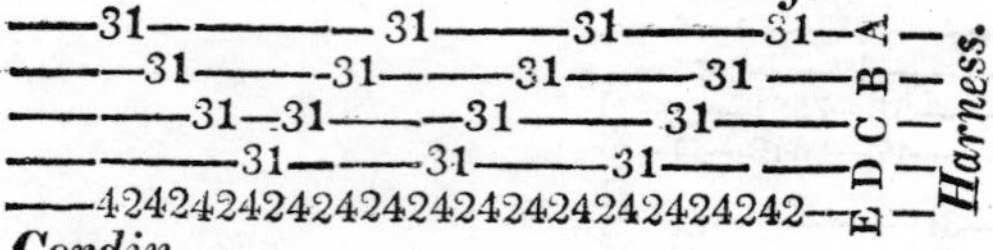

31 31 31 31 A
31 31 31 31 B
31 31 31 31 C
31 31 31 D
4242424242424242424242424242424242 E

Harness.

Cording.

Lams.

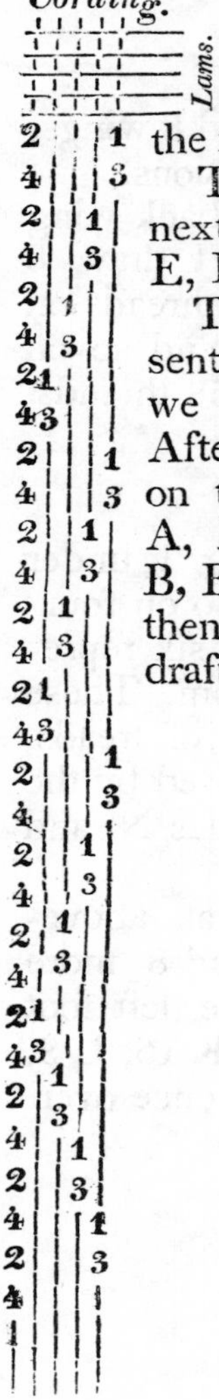

This pattern is formed with 5 treadles, and 5 wings. Half of the threads are drawn on the front wing E.

The first thread is drawn on wing A, fig, 1, next on E, next on A, E, B, E, B, E, C, E, C, E, D, E, D, E, and so on, drawing 88 threads.

This draft for want of room, does not represent but 60 threads; but it will be found that we have described the remainder by letters. After you have drawn the 60 threads, continue on thus, D, E, D, E, C, E, C, E, B, E, B, E, A, E, A, E, D, E, D, E, C, E, C, E, B, E, B, E: the whole of the draft is now through; then begin again at fig. 1, on wing A, where the draft first commenced.

Explanation of Cording and Tread for No. 22.

In the cording there are 20 long cords for the short lams, and 5 short cords for the long lams.

TREAD.

The first tread is on treadle F, fig. 1, under the cording: next on J, fig. 2, next F, J, G, J, G, J, H, J, H, J, I, J, I, J, and so on, treading 88 treads.

This draft, for want of room, does not represent but 60 treads, but we have, as in the drawing, described the remainder by letters.

After treading the 60 treads continue through thus; I, J, I, J, H, J, H, J, G, J, G, J, F, J, F, J, I, J, I, J, H, J, H, J, G, J, G, J; the whole of the draft of the tread is now through. Begin again on F, fig. 1. under the cording as before.

While you are weaving, the left foot is always on treadle J, which forms the plain part of the cloth, and the other four form the flower.

The slaie for this pattern, should be 2 beers finer than for plain cloth, and drawn 2 threads in a reed.

No. 23, Block Stripe Diaper.

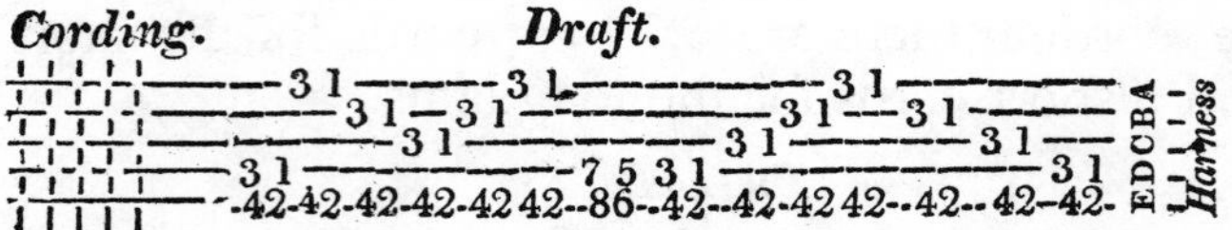

Cording. *Draft.*

```
------31------31-----------31------------  A
---------31--31-----------31---31--------  B
------------31-----------31---------31---  C
---31-----------7531-----------------31--  D
-42-42-42-42-4242--86--42--42-4242--42--42-42-  E
                                        Harness
```

```
2       1
4       3
2     1
4     3
2   1
4   3
21
43
2       1
4       3
J I H G F
treadles.
```

This pattern is formed with 5 treadles and 5 wings. Half of the threads are drawn on the front wing E. The first thread is drawn on wing D, fig. 1. next on E, next on D, E, C, E, C, E, and so on through the draft, which is once over, when you will begin again on D, as before.

There are 12 long cords for short lams, and 13 short cords for the long lams.

TREAD.

The first tread is on F, fig. 1, under the cording, next on J, fig. 2, next on F, J, G, J, G, J, and so on until once over, as directed in the draft of treading; then begin again on F, as before.

When you are weaving, the left foot is always on treadle J. The treadles which form the plain cloth are F, and J, and the others form the flower.

The slaie for this pattern, should be two beers finer than for plain cloth, and draw two threads in a reed.

No. 24, Birds Eye Carpet.

Cording. *Draft.*

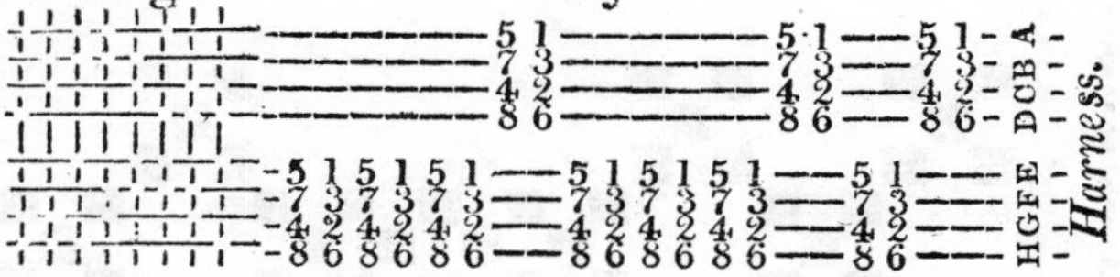

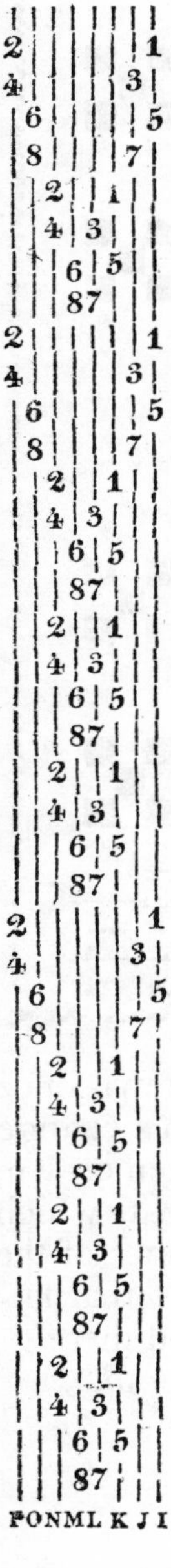

```
——————5 1——————5 1——5 1- A -
——————7 3——————7 3——7 3- B -
——————4 2——————4 2——4 2- C -
——————8 6——————8 6——8 6- D -
-5 1 5 1 5 1——5 1 5 1 5 1——5 1——— E -
-7 3 7 3 7 3——7 3 7 3 7 3——7 3——— F -
-4 2 4 2 4 2——4 2 4 2 4 2——4 2——— G -
-8 6 8 6 8 6——8 6 8 6 8 6——8 6——— H -
```

Harness.

This pattern is formed with eight treadles, and 8 wings. The wings are represented as being in two divisions, with 4 wings in each. You will now begin, by drawing the first thread on the back division, wing A, fig. 1: next draw on C, B, C, A, D, B, D; commence next on the front division, wing E, then G, F, G, E, H, F, H; begin again on the back division, wing A, and so on through the draft. Then begin on the back wing A, as first directed, observing that it takes 80 threads to draw the figure once over.

There are 32 long cords, for short lams, and 32 short cords for long lams.

TREAD.

The first tread is on treadle I, begun at fig. 1, near the cording; next tread P, fig. 2, then J, P, I, O, J, O, which makes 8 treads: then K, N, L, N, K, M, L, M, making 16 treads; you will then continue to tread all the draft of treading through, being in the whole figure 80 treads; it is then begun on I again, fig. 1, on the top as before.

PONML K J I

No. 25, Rose and Compass Diaper.

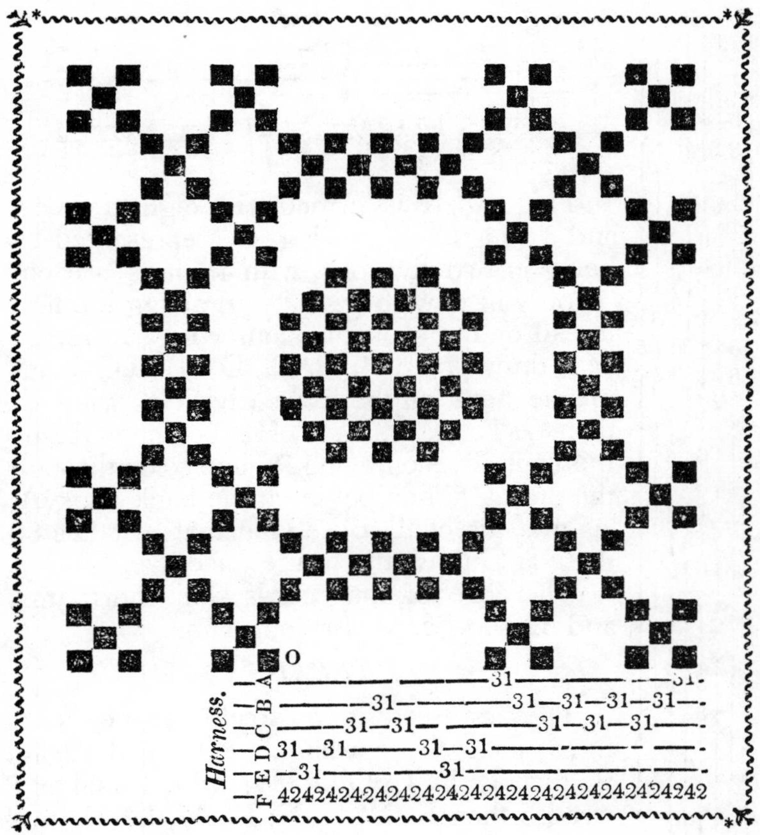

This draft represents the figure as being drawn once over. There is on it 18 changes, 4 figures to a change as 1, 2, 3, 4. The four figures or threads, when drawn, make one block, and 18 blocks from the right, which extend only to O on the plate, is all that the draft of the harness represents. The blocks to the left of that letter, is the figure commenced again, and placed there to make the plate appear square, as it is in the cloth.

No. 25, Cording and Tread.

Cording.

Lams.

L	K	J	I	H	G
2				1	
4				3	
2					1
4					3
2				1	
4				3	
2			1		
4			3		
2		1			
4		3			
2			1		
4			3		
2				1	
4				3	
2					1
4					3
2				1	
4				3	
2			1		
4			3		
2		1			
4					
2	1				
4	3				
2		1			
4		3			
2	1				
4	3				
2		1			
4		3			
2	1				
4	3				
2		1			
4		3			
2			1		
4			3		

Treadles

In the cording there are 16 long cords on the short lams, and 20 short cords on the long lams.

TREAD.

The first tread is on treadle H, fig. 1, next on L, fig. 2, next H, L, G, L, G, L, and so on until the tread is through as directed, being in the whole, 72 treads. While you are weaving the left foot is always on the left hand treadle L, which makes the plain part of the cloth, while the rest form the flower. The slaie for this pattern, should be 2 beers finer than for plain cloth, and draw 2 threads in a reed.

Explanation of the draft No. 25.

This pattern has 6 wings. Draw the first thread on the back wing A, fig. 1, next on wing F, next on A, F, B, F, B, F, and so on, as the draft directs. Half of the threads are drawn on wing F, being 72 threads in the figure.

No. 26, Plain Block Carpet.

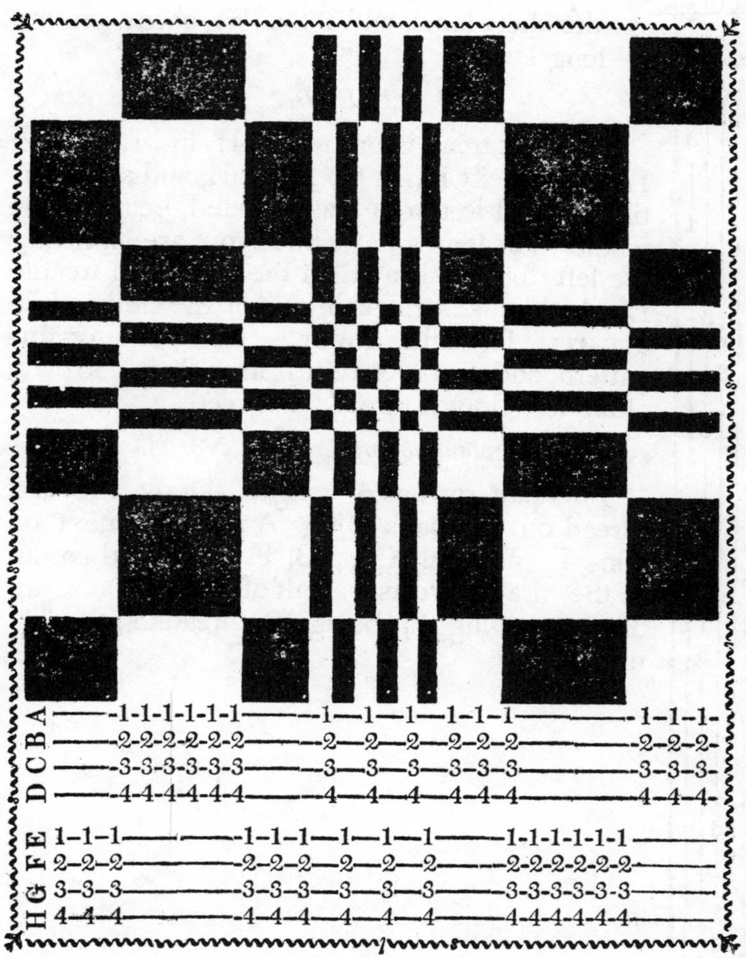

Explanation of Draft and Plate No. 26.

This pattern is formed with 8 treadles, and 8 wings. The wings are represented as being in two divisions with 4 in each.

Begin to draw on the back division wing A, fig. 1, drawing 12 threads on A, B, C, D, and so on as the draft directs, drawing 120 threads, the last thread being drawn on H. You will now proceed to draw the threads for the small blocks, that appear in the center of the plate a second time over, thus draw 4 threads on the 4 back wings A, B, C, D, then four threads on the 4 front wings, then 4 on the 4 back wings, next 4 on the 4 front wings, then 4 on the 4 back wings, and 4 on the 4 front wings. The draft is now through; although the plate from want of room, does not represent the whole figure, as will appear in the cloth. You will now commence drawing the whole draft the second time over, beginning the 12 threads A, B, C, D, as at first.

No. 26. Cording and Tread.

```
PONMLK J I
24 | | | | 31
24 | | | | 31
24 | | | | 31
| | 2431 | |
| | 6875 | |
| | 2431 | |
| | 6875 | |
| | 2431 | |
| | 6875 | |
24 | | | | 31
24 | | | | 31
24 | | | | 31
| | 2431 | |
24 | | | | 31
| | 2431 | |
24 | | | | 31
| | 2431 | |
24 | | | | 31
| | 2431 | |
| | 2431 | |
| | 2431 | |
24 | | | | 31
24 | | | | 31
24 | | | | 31
24 | | | | 31
24 | | | | 31
24 | | | | 31
| | 2431 | |
| | 2431 | |
| | 2431 | |
24 | | | | 31
| | 2431 | |
24 | | | | 31
| | 2431 | |
24 | | | | 31
| | 2431 | |
| | | | | | | |
Treadles.
```

Cording.

Lams.

In the cording there are 32 long cords, and 32 short cords.

TREAD.

The first tread is on treadle I, fig. 1, next on P, fig. 2, next on J, O, I, P, J, O, I, P, J, O, this finishes the first change: you will now tread on the second change, K, N, L, M, and so on, treading as many treads as the draft directs, being 144 treads; it is then begun again as before.

No. 27, Damask Diaper.

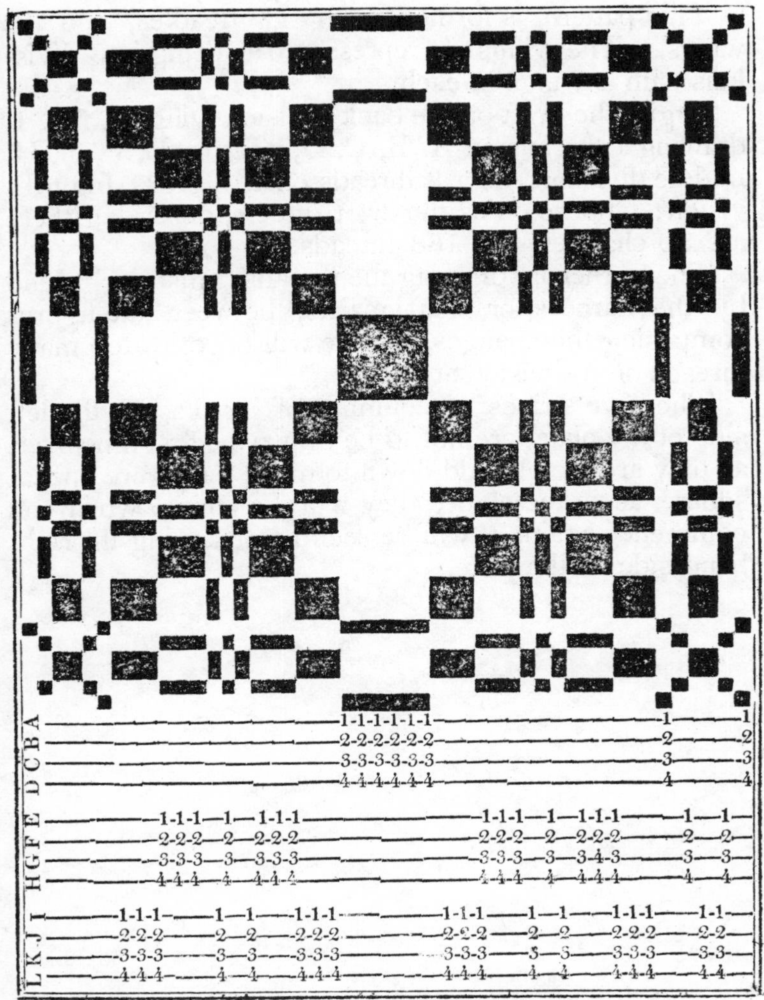

Explanation of Draft No 27.

This pattern is formed with 12 treadles, and 12 wings. The wings are represented as being in 3 divisions with 4 wings in each.

Begin the draft on the back division wing A, fig. 1, drawing 4 threads on A, B, C, D, next on E, F, G, H, middle division; next 8 threads on I, J, K, L, front division: and so on as the draft directs, observing there are 20 changes, and 168 threads.

The learner in drawing the threads, must be guided by the harness, or shaft marks, between the figures composing the changes, that he will not draw too many threads on a division at once.

The five stripes or columns of blocks, on the left side of the plate, are not to be drawn the first time over, as they are merely laid down to make the figure appear square, as in the cloth; they will be drawn when you commence again, as will be seen by observing the right hand side of the plate.

Cording and Tread, of No. 27.

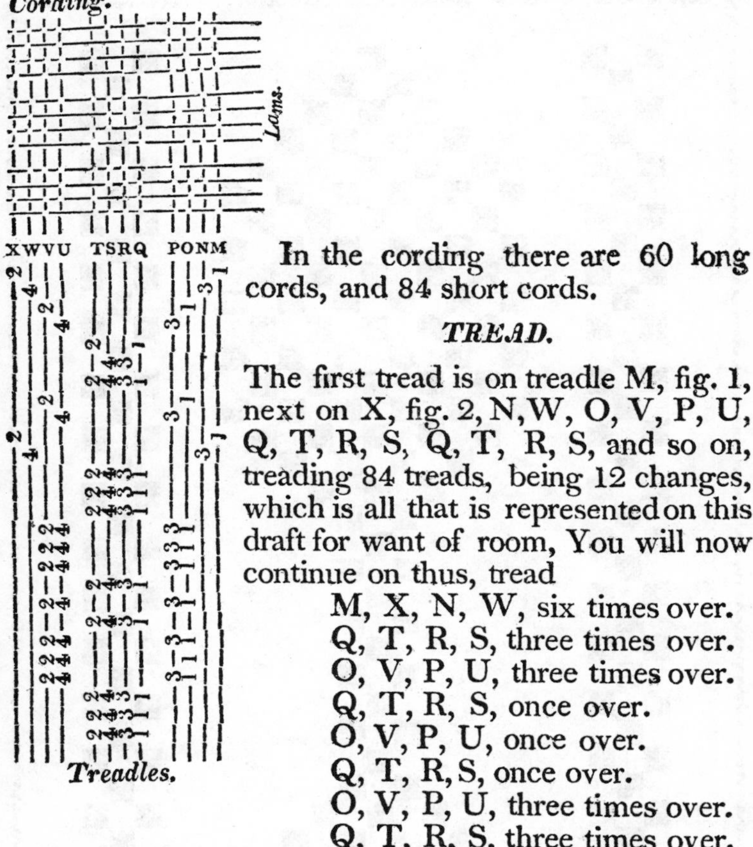

In the cording there are 60 long cords, and 84 short cords.

TREAD.

The first tread is on treadle M, fig. 1, next on X, fig. 2, N, W, O, V, P, U, Q, T, R, S, Q, T, R, S, and so on, treading 84 treads, being 12 changes, which is all that is represented on this draft for want of room, You will now continue on thus, tread

M, X, N, W, six times over.
Q, T, R, S, three times over.
O, V, P, U, three times over.
Q, T, R, S, once over.
O, V, P, U, once over.
Q, T, R, S, once over.
O, V, P, U, three times over.
Q, T, R, S, three times over.

The figure is now trod once through when you will begin again as at first.

No. 28 Curtain Diaper.

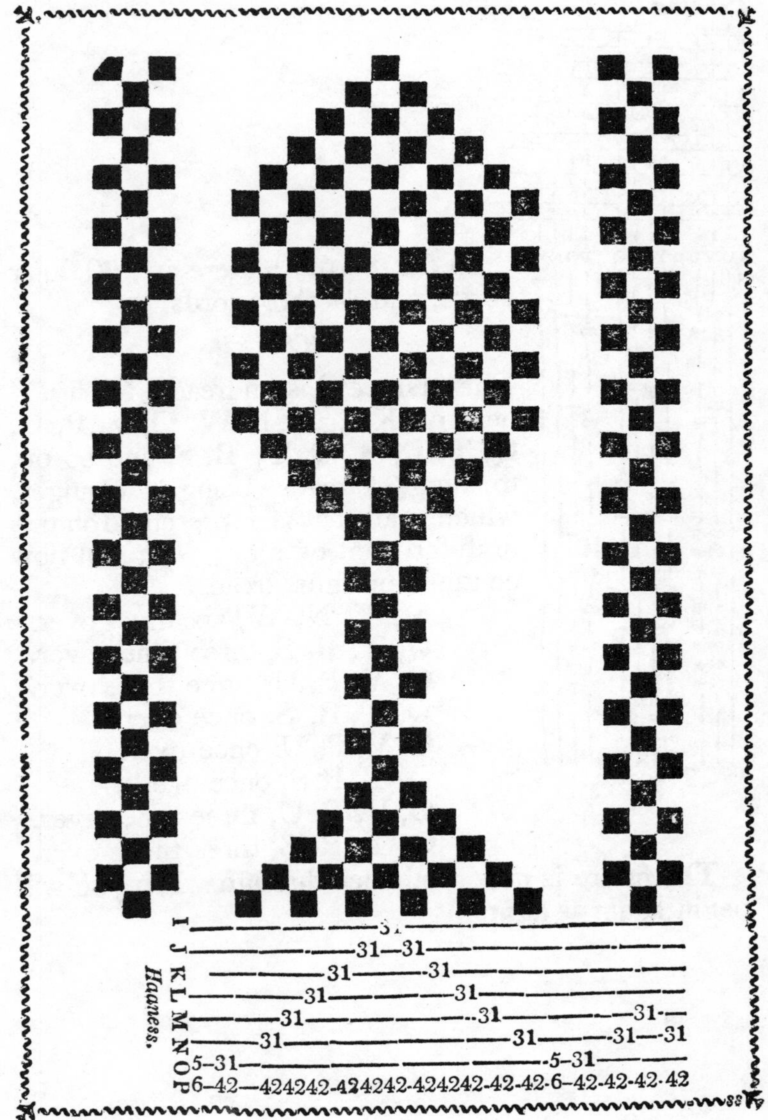

Explanation of Draft No. 28.

This pattern is formed with 8 treadles, and 8 wings. Half of the threads are drawn in the front wing P.

Draw the first thread on wing N, fig. 1, next on P, fig. 2, N, P, M, P, M, P, N, P, N, P, O, P, O, P, O, P, and so on, as directed through the draft, being 68 threads on the figure, you will then begin again as before. The left hand pillar in the plate, merely represents the first pillar as being drawn the second time. The draft or drawing therefore, does not extend only to that pillar.

In the cording to No. 28, there are 26 long cords on short lams, and 38 short cords on long lams.

Explanation of Tread for No. 28,

In the first place the learner will observe the draft of treading is represented in two parts for want of room and will perceive that by supposing the right hand colums to be placed directly under those of the left, it will appear correct and of the same shape as one side of the main pillar of the plate.

Should he wish to have a plain bar on the top of the pillars, he will tread A, H, three times each as represented on the top of the draft.

Begin the tread on B, fig. 1, right hand column; next H, fig. 2, next B, H, and so on extending upwards, until at the top of the columns. You will observe that the tread must be continued on to D, in the left hand colums, and extend upwards as directed until through, when you will commence again on the right hand colums as before. Should the weaver while weaving, wish to form a different figure from the one represented in the plate, he can form one that will appear well, by merely changing the tread. After treading the twentieth change from the beginning, which is C, go on thus—D, E, F, E, D, C, B, C, D, E, F, G: then begin on the other colums and go over the second time as at first directed. While you are weaving, the left foot is always on treadle H. Use a slaie 2 beers finer than for plain cloth and draw 2 threads in a reed.

Cording and Tread of No. 28.

Lamr,

H	G	F	E	D	C	B	A
6							5
4							3
2							1
4	3						
2	1						
4		3					
2		1					
4			3				
2			1				
4				3			
2				1			
4					3		
2					1		
4						3	
2						1	
4					3		
2					1		
4						3	
2						1	
4					3		
2					1		
4						3	
2						1	
4					3		
2					1		
4						3	
2						1	
4					3		
2					1		
4						3	
2						1	
4					3		
2					1		
4				3			
2				1			

HGFEDCBA

H	G	F	E	D	C	B	A
4			3				
2			1				
4		3					
2		1					
4	3						
2	1						
4		3					
2		1					
4	3						
2	1						
4		3					
2		1					
4	3						
2	1						
4		3					
2		1					
4	3						
2	1						
4		3					
2		1					
4	3						
2	1						
4		3					
2		1					
4			3				
2			1				
4				3			
2				1			
4					3		
2					1		
4						3	
2						1	

HGFEDCBA

Treadles.

No. 29, Block Carpet.

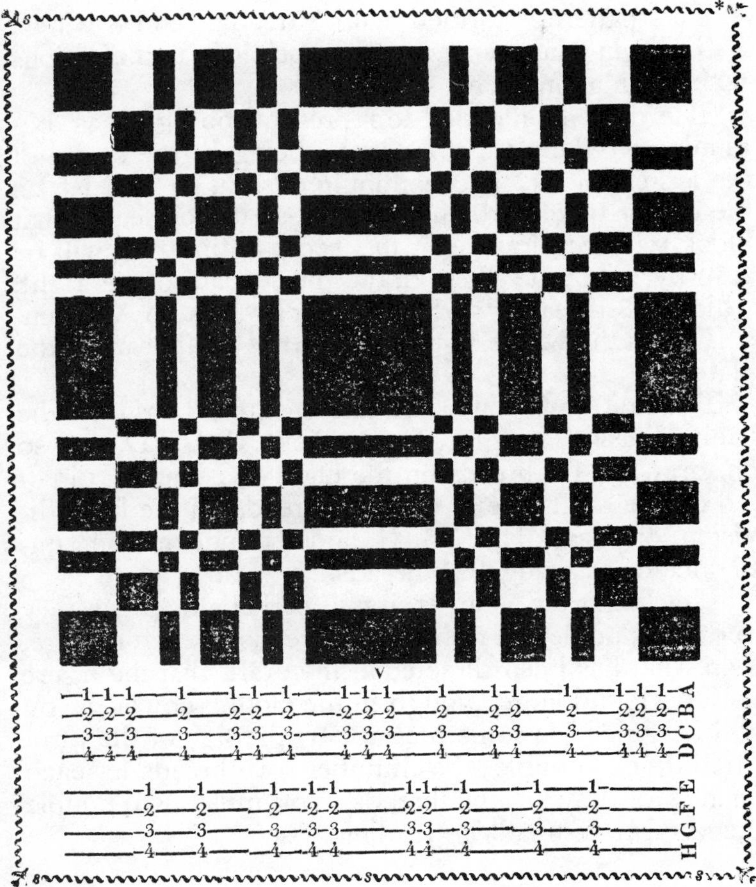

Explanation of Draft and Plate No. 29.

This pattern is formed with 8 treadles and 8 wings.

The wings are represented as being in two divisions with 4 wings in each.

The draft is intended to represent the figure as beginning on the plate at letter V, being in the centre of the largest block, and continuing as far to the left as the corner block, which it includes; it then leaves that block without drawing it the second time, as will be seen by the draft; then draw the second to the right, which is 8 threads, and so on backwards to V again.

This is the whole figure though not as appears in the plate.

The first thread will be drawn thus; begin on the back division, wing A, fig. 1, next B, C, D, and so on, drawing 12 threads on the back division, as directed on the draft; next draw 4 threads on the front division, on wings E, F, G, H, and continue drawing until once over, being 108 threads.

This being for a carpet, it will perhaps be necessary to draw double the number of threads in each change, than what has been directed in the draft, that the figure may be found large enough in the cloth: however you will be guided in some measure by the size of the yarn. Should you double the number of threads in each change of drawing the threads, you must also double the number of treads in treading.

No. 29, Cording and Tread.

Cording.

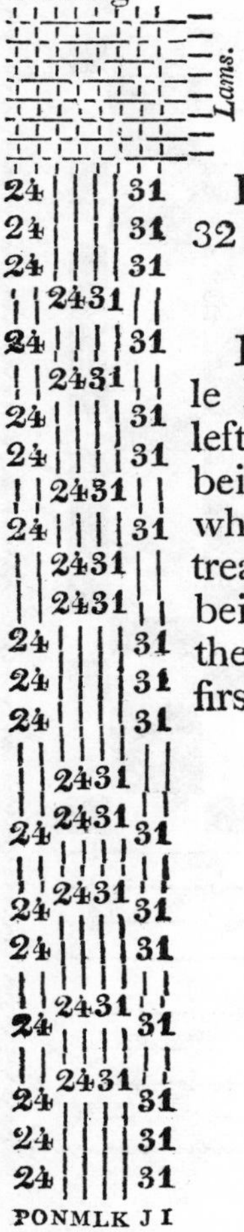

Lams.

24 31
24 31
24 31
2431
24 31
2431
24 31
24 31
2431
24 31
2431
2431
24 31
24 31
24 31
2431
24 2431 31
24 2431 31
24 31
24 2431 31
24 2431 31
24 31
24 31

PONMLK J I
Treadles.

In the cording, there are 32 long cords and 32 short cords.

TREAD.

Begin the tread with the right foot on treadle I, fig. 1, under the cording, next with the left foot on P, fig. 2, and so on for 12 treads, being one change; next on K, N, L, M, which is the second change; then continue treading through as the treadle draft directs, being 17 changes, and 108 treads to complete the figure. You will then begin again as at first.

No. 30, Birds Eye Carpet.

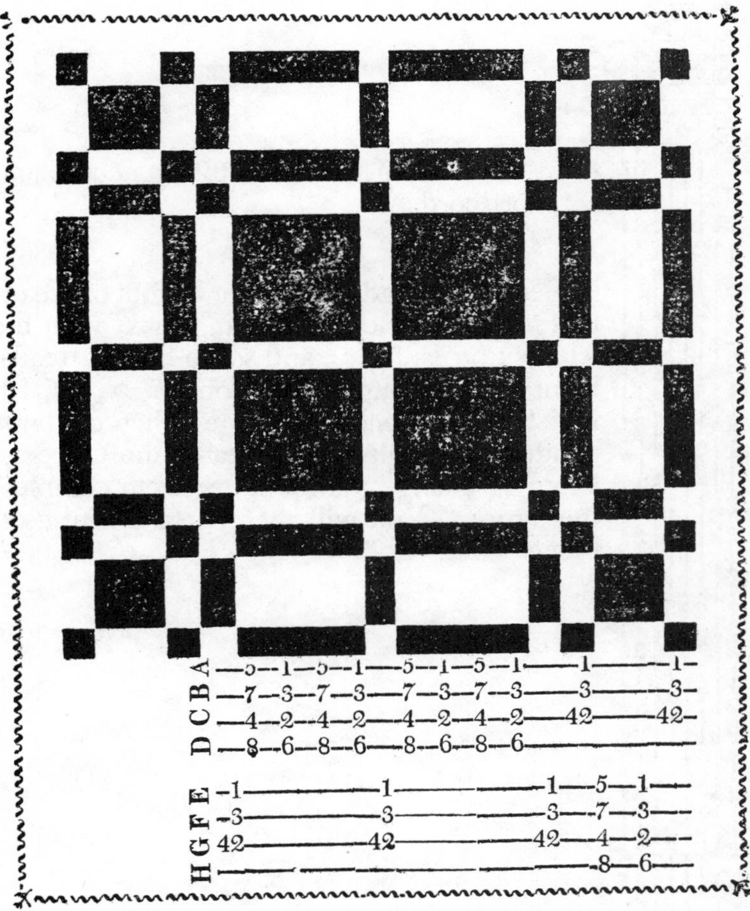

Explanation of Draft No. 30.

This pattern is formed with 8 treadles, and 8 wings: the wings are represented as being in two divisions, with 4 wings in each.

Draw the first thread on the back division, wing A, fig. 1, next on C, fig. 2, next on B, then C, which forms one change, next draw on the front division, wings E, G, F, G, E, H, F, H, and so on through, as the draft directs, being 60 threads in the figure. You will then begin again as at first.

The three stripes or colums of blocks, on the left side of the plate, are not to be drawn the first time over, as they are merely laid down to make the figure appear square, like the cloth: they will be drawn when you commence again, as will be seen by observing the right hand side of the plate.

Cording and Tread for No. 30.

Cording.

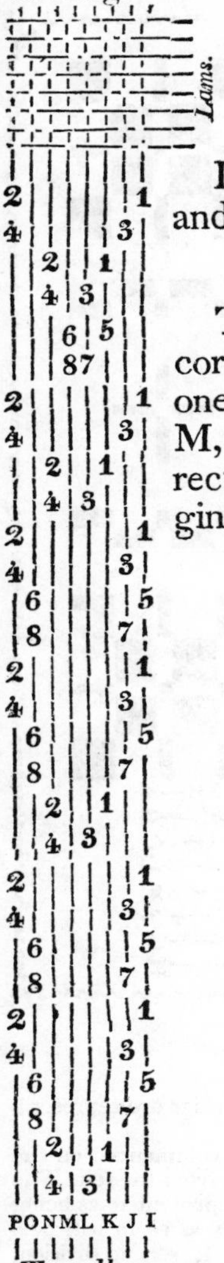

Lams.

PONMLKJI

Treadles.

In the cording there are 32 long cords, and 32 short cords.

TREAD.

The first tread is on I, fig. 1, under the cording; next on P, fig. 2, J, P, which is one change; next on K, N, L, N, K, M, L, M, and so on through the whole draft as directed, being 60 treads. You will then begin on I, fig. 1, as at first.

No. 31, Cross and Circle Coverlet.

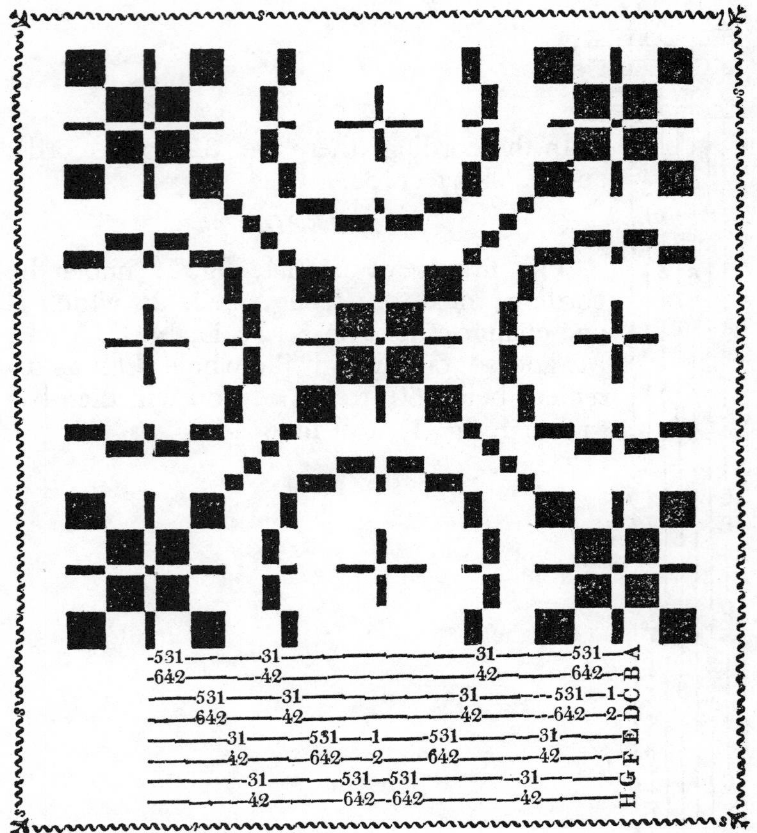

Explanation of Draft No. 31.

This pattern is formed with 6 treadles, and 8 wings. The wings are represented as being in 4 divisions, with 2 wings in each.

The learner will observe, that the drawing of the threads is commenced on the third stripe or block of the plate, and ends on the fourth stripe from the left. The blocks on the right, and left side of the plate, that are not represented as being drawn, are placed there merely to exhibit the figure (as nearly as room will permit) in the cloth. The first thread is drawn on wing C, fig. 1, second division, next on D, fig. 2, and so on until the draft is through, being 82 threads, then begin again as at first.

Cording and Tread for No. 31

Cording.

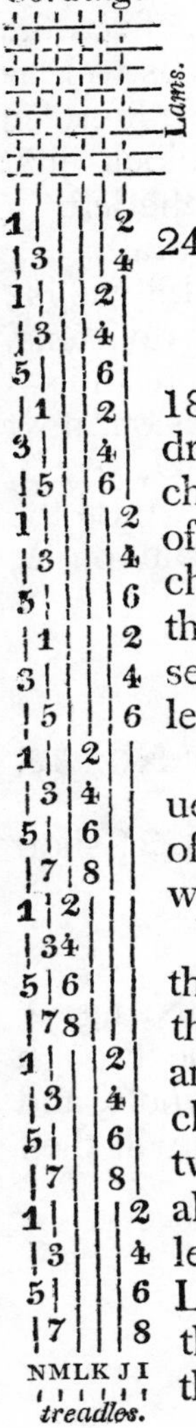

Lams.

NMLK J I

treadles.

In the cording there are 24 long cords, and 24 short cords.

TREAD.

In the whole tread of this pattern, there are 18 changes, being the same number as in the drawing of the threads. There are only 7 changes represented in the treadle draft for want of room; these seven, as also the rest of the changes, have double the number of treads than there are threads in the drawing: this is caused by the binding yarn, which is trod by treadles N, M,

It will be observed that the left foot is continued on treadles N, M, through the whole draft of treading, which is 84 treads, and 84 treads with the right foot also.

Begin the tread on treadle N, fig. 1, under the cording, next right foot on I, fig. 2, M, I, this is one change or 4 treads: next on N, J, and so on 16 treads, which is the second change. Next tread with the right foot on I, twelve treads, K, 8, L, 8, J, 8, I, 8: this makes all the changes that are represented on the treadles; then continue K, 12 treads, L, 12, K, 4, L, 12, K, 12, I, 8, J, 8, L, 8, K, 8, I, 12, J, 12; the whole treading in the draft or figure is now through, being 168 treads.

Explanation of Draft and Plate No. 32.

This draft represents the figure as being once drawn over; it takes two thirds of the third block, from the right, (the white spaces being called blocks as well as those that are black,) and continues to the left, fourteen changes. As you take only a part of the block first mentioned, and a part of the third, from the left, it makes but one block, as will be seen by the draft.

The pattern is formed with 6 treadles and 8 wings; the wings are represented as being in four divisions, with two wings in each. The draft is begun thus—first thread drawn on wing A, fig. 1, back division, next on B, fig. 2, next on A, B, C, D, C, D, C, D, A, B, A, B, A, B, E, F, G, H, E, F, and so on until the draft is once over, when you will begin again on A, fig. 1, as at first; 48 threads form the figure.

Explanation of Cording and Tread for No. 32.

In the cording there are 24 long cords and 24 short cords.

TREAD.

The first tread is on treadle I, fig. 1, next N, fig. 2, J, N, I, N, J, N, which is one change; continue through as the draft directs, being 15 changes in the whole, and 96 treads, which completes the figure; you will then begin again as at first on treadle I, fig. 1.

No. 32, Eight Shaft Coverlet,

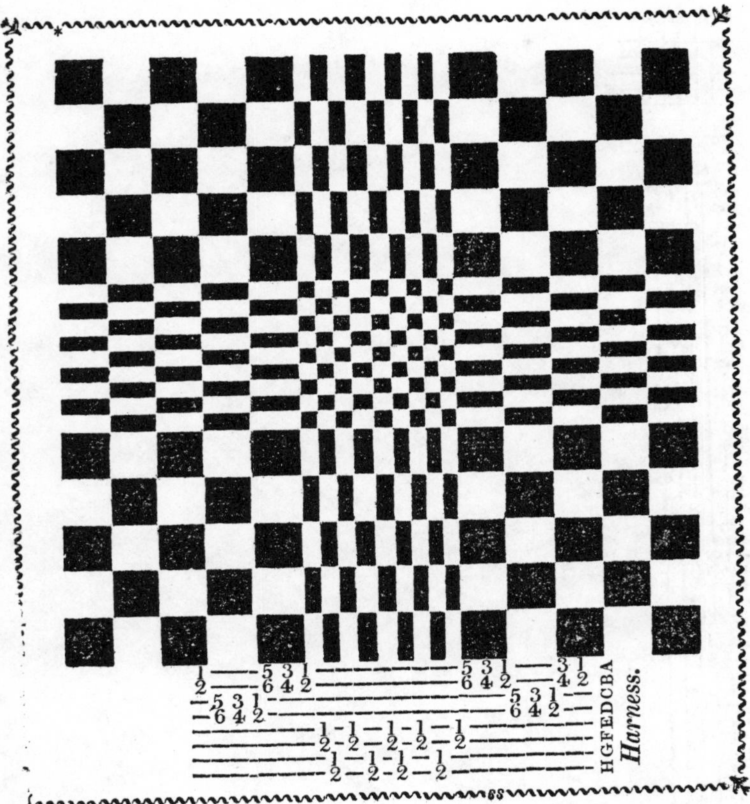

Cording and Tread, of No. 32.

Cording.

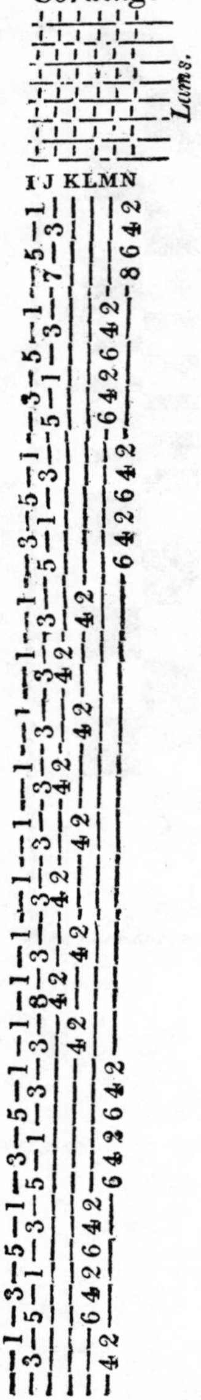

Lams.

I J KLMN

1—5—1—5—3—1—5—3—1—1—1—1—1—1—1—1—1—1—5—3—1—5—3—1

3—7—3—1—5—3—1—5—3—3—3—3—3—3—3—8—3—3—1—5—3—1—5—3

42—42—42—42—42

42—42—42—42—42—642642

8642—642642—642642—642642—42

No. 33. Broad Cloth.

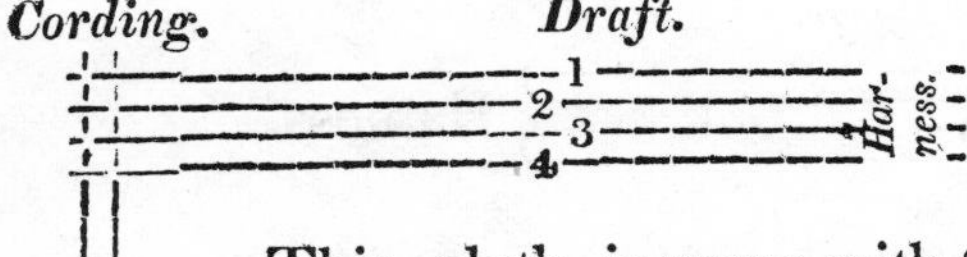

This cloth is wove with 2 treadles, and four wings in the harness; and has 4 long cords that connect the short lams and treadles, and 4 short cords that are fixed to the long lams and treadles. The draft is represented as being drawn over once. First drawn thread is on the back wing, figure 1, then 2, 3, 4. You will then begin again on the back wing as before, and so proceed until all the threads are drawn. In the treading, figure 1 is for the right foot and figure 2 for the left.

Twenty eight pounds of woollen yarn should warp 63 yards, or in that proportion; let the fineness be 2½, 3, 3½, 4 or 4½ runs to the pound.

Twenty-eight pounds 4½ runs to the pound, 63 yards, 80 beers, eleven quarters wide.

28 lbs. 4 runs to the pound, 63 yards, 72 beers, 10½ quarters wide.

28 lbs. 3½ runs to the pound, 63 yards, 62 beers, 10 quarters wide.

28 lbs. 3 runs to the pound, 63 yards, 54 beers, 9½ quarters wide.

28 lbs. 2½ runs to the pound, 63 yards, 45 beers, 9 quarters wide.

For further explanation, see subject of woollen weaving.

No. 34. Casimere.

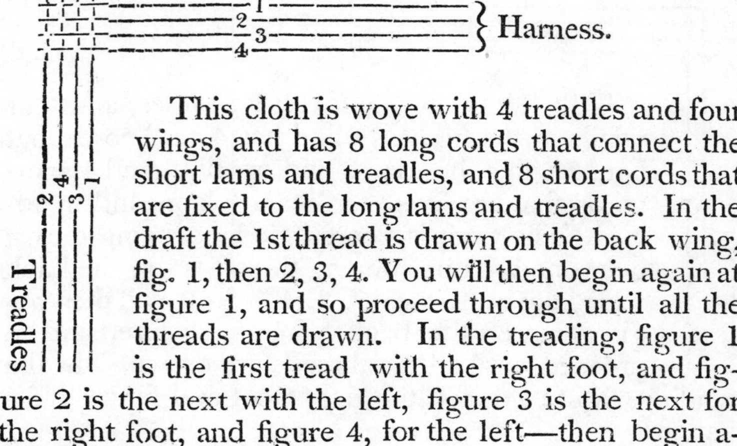

This cloth is wove with 4 treadles and four wings, and has 8 long cords that connect the short lams and treadles, and 8 short cords that are fixed to the long lams and treadles. In the draft the 1st thread is drawn on the back wing, fig. 1, then 2, 3, 4. You will then begin again at figure 1, and so proceed through until all the threads are drawn. In the treading, figure 1 is the first tread with the right foot, and figure 2 is the next with the left, figure 3 is the next for the right foot, and figure 4, for the left—then begin again on figure 1.

The two kinds of Casimere, single and double milled, are wove in the same way : the difference is made in the filling.

The double milled should be made of slack filling, and the single milled of twist, nearly the same as the warp.

Fifteen pounds five runs to the pound is sufficient for a warp of sixty-three yards long—48 beers in the harness, 24 reed, 4 threads in a split—5 quarters wide.

No. 35. Satinet.

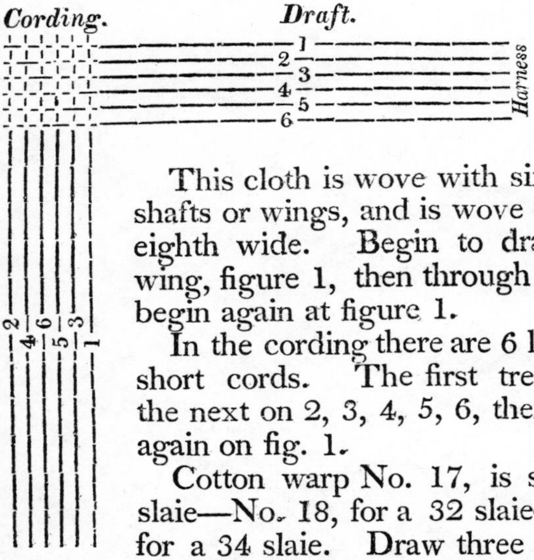

Cording. *Draft.*

1 2 3 4 5 6 *Harness*

2 4 6 5 3 1

This cloth is wove with six treadles and six shafts or wings, and is wove one yard and one eighth wide. Begin to draw on the back wing, figure 1, then through 2, 3, 4, 5, 6, then begin again at figure 1.

In the cording there are 6 long cords and 30 short cords. The first tread is on figure 1, the next on 2, 3, 4, 5, 6, then begin the tread again on fig. 1.

Cotton warp No. 17, is suitable for a 30 slaie—No. 18, for a 32 slaie—No's. 19 & 20 for a 34 slaie. Draw three threads in a split, and fill with slack twisted woollen yarn, three runs to the pound.

DYEING OF COTTON.

Remarks and Directions on Preparing and Dying Cotton Yarn.

In the first place we will notice that cotton yarn must be well cleansed, by making it free from its natural oil, before it can be dyed in a complete manner. Before this is done, it is necessary for the yarn to be put in a proper form. We shall therefore now give directions to prepare the yarn for boiling.

Take a 5 pound bundle of cotton yarn, and form the whole into links or a chain, which is done in the following manner; after first taking notice that for coarse yarn you will take about 3 skeins for a link, but yarn that is No. 14 or finer, take 6 skeins.

First take 3 skeins and place them together at whole length, then take three more and pass through the first, and double the last; then three more are to be put through the two loops of the last, and so on until you have made 5 pounds into a chain, taking one of the skeins to loop through the last end to secure it.

Those dyers who color yarn for manufacturing establishments, or for others in large quantities, will find it necessary to mark the yarn, so that each kind may be kept separate, and returned in a regular manner; indeed this plan must be adopted as a rule; for it will be found impossible to keep the different numbers separate without; especially in boiling different numbers at once.

We shall now give directions to mark the yarn as we have practiced, which will be easily understood.—First take a piece of strong twine about a foot long, and put it through the loop of the last skein in the linked chain; then draw both ends of the twine together, and make a knot with both branches of the twine near the loop of the yarn. This knot made with both branches of the twine, you will always count or call as 10, and answers for No. 10 yarn. Should a bundle of yarn be No. 12, then you must make one large knot, and two small knots on the single branch of the twine, as the small knots count one each, and the large ones 10 each. If your yarn is No. 20, make two large knots. If it is No. 22, make two large knots and two small ones; in this way you can mark any number you wish, which mark will keep on through the operations of boiling, dyeing and drying.

After your yarn is all chained up and marked for one boiling, you will then prepare your boiler with a sufficient quantity of water to cover your yarn while boiling. After the water has arrived at a scalding heat, for every 5 pounds of yarn, put in half an ounce of pearlash; when it is dissolved, put in your yarn and boil it well for about five or six hours, adding water occasionally.

The yarn is next to be taken out and cooled so that you will be able to take the links apart with your hands; as you take the links apart, you will count it off into pound bunches, and put 5 pounds of one number on 5 sticks, and those 5 sticks to be kept together; in this way proceed with the rest, observing to examine the twine in the first place, to be sure of the number before you begin to count it off.

After you have counted it all off and placed the yarn on the sticks, you will then rinse it, by taking 5 pounds at a time and turning it in a half hogshead nearly full of water, resting the sticks on two narrow strips of board which are placed on the top of the tub. When you have turned the yarn for five minutes, take another strip of board which you must have handy, and place across the two other strips; then bring up one pound of yarn at a time, until you put up the 5 pounds; then let it drain, and proceed with the rest in the same manner.

In the next place the yarn is to be wrung and shook out with care, minding not to break it. Cotton yarn is wrung in different ways, sometimes on a wringing machine, and in some dye houses on a pin fixed horizontally into a post; this last manner of wringing has one advantage over the other which is this; the yarn is continually kept on the dye sticks. Care must be observed to keep each five pounds together through all the operations of rincing, wringing, dyeing and drying, which is very easy after a little practice.

Cotton yarn is dyed on sticks, which are about two feet in length and about one inch in diameter ,but sometimes little more where the yarn is wrung on the stick and pin. Dye sticks should be made of hard wood that is not liable to get rough, as they should be entirely smooth to prevent injuring the yarn while you are wringing, shaking out, or turning it in the dye.

In dyeing most colors on cotton yarn in dye houses, (excepting indigo blue) 20 sticks are used, and generally one pound is put on each stick, which are rested on two narrow slips of boards over a tub or half hogshead. The yarn is then turned one pound after another in the dye liquor, a longer or shorter time as occasion requires.

In dyeing almost every kind of color on cotton, you will have your dyes no hotter than you can endure your hand in while dipping the yarn.

The yarn is commonly received from factories in 5 pound bundles, and is to be returned in the same quantity in a bundle, but not generally in the same manner. The most common method has been to dry 5 pounds on a pole, having the number marked on the pole with chalk, which is done soon as the yarn is dyed; this is done for the sake of convenience in many cases; but should there be a failure in marking the number with chalk, or should it get rubbed off, still the marked twine on one of the skeins for every 5 pounds, will distinguish the right number.

After the yarn is dry, for instance, a pole containing 5 pounds of No. 12, you will begin and collect 12 skeins with your right hand, by slipping them into the left: in taking the last skein of the twelve, you will slip it through the rest, and make a noose or loop, which makes a pound bunch, and so proceed with any other numbers, either warp or filling. You will then take the five looped skeins that secure the pound bunches and slip them off the pole and twist them a little together, and when you carry the yarn into a room, lay it down and mark the number with chalk near it. When you put up each 5 pounds lay it lengthwise and save out 2 skeins to bind it; then put a printed or written ticket on it explaining the number.

By following this method of putting up yarn in pound bunches, it will save manufacturers who put out pieces to weave, a great deal of time, especially if the dyer is faithful in counting the yarn right.

In making out pieces to weavers, it is essential that the warp is counted exact. Some manufacturers count the warp over after the dyer, to be convinced that it is exact, but not the filling, where it is put up in pound bunches.

Observations on Preparing and Dyeing Cotton Yarn in small quantities, calculated for families.

In preparing small quantities of yarn for boiling, we recommend to make it into a chain; which method will be found described in the first part of the first remarks; also the manner of marking the yarn and boiling it.

It will first be noticed that cotton yarn for all colors is to be dyed on sticks, having the sticks placed on the top of a tub or kettle while turning the yarn, each stick containing one pound. Families will not often have occasion to use large tubs or kettles in dyeing cotton. In using small ones, it will be found inconvenient to wring a pound of yarn over them; therefore when you wring the yarn, either the first time after being rinsed, or in the course of dyeing, you will wring only 2 or 3 skeins at a time; it is then to be shook out straight and placed in a separate manner on the sticks.

Directions will now be given to prepare a tub or kettle to die 5 pounds of yarn. A half barrel tub, or kettle that will contain nearly as much liquor, will be large enough to die 5 pounds. In this case you will have 5 sticks, with a pound on a stick. The yarn is to be put in the dye all at once, and turned as long a time as will be hereafter mentioned in the receipts.

Should you color less than 5 pounds, your tub or kettle may be small in proportion, and observe that your dye for cotton must be as warm as you can bear the hand in while dipping the yarn. When you wring the yarn out of the dye, first move the sticks one side of the tub or kettle, taking one small parcel off from the stick at a time until all of it is wrung; then shake it out and place it on the sticks as before.

We recommend to all families who often have occasion to dry white or colored yarn, to use smooth poles, having the yarn hung the whole length of the skein; in this way yarn will dry not only more even and quicker, but keep in better order for weaving.

N. B. Where families want to boil out cotton yarn, they can use soap suds instead of pearl ash, if they like.

Observations on boiling Dye Woods.

It will not be improper to observe that when any kind of wood whatever is used in dyeing, it must first be cut into small shavings or chips, and put loosely into a thin coarse bag, that it may not stick to the woollen cloth or yarn, as the rough chips will not only tear the goods, but cloud or blot them in those places where they stick. N. B. Observe always to have a plenty of dye liquor, so that your cloth and yarn may be dyed even.

When chips are boiled up for dyeing cotton, the chips must be allowed to settle at the bottom of the kettle, then pour the clear part off into a tub; this is where the chips are not put in a bag. Families that have no spare kettles can put the chips into a bag, and use the same kettle for dipping the cotton. Should they put in the chips loose in the dye to boil, they can strain it through a clean basket, or very coarse open wove cloth. In all cases cotton yarn must be dyed in a clear dye free from any chips.

On vats used in dyeing blue on cotton & linen.

The vats used in dyeing blue on cotton and linen in the cold dye, are of various kinds and sizes, such as rum hogsheads, brandy pipes, and pine vats. The last kind are usually made particularly for dyeing, and should be of the best white pine plank thoroughly seasoned, sound and entirely free from knots. The staves should be at least one inch and a quarter thick when finished, and bound with iron hoops.

Iron bound hogsheads are generally used at most dye houses from being so easily procured; they will answer very well to color cotton yarn in once a day, but will not do for linen, as the skeins of linen being so long would disturb the sediment of the dye; therefore the vats intended for dyeing linen should be made taller in proportion. The top of such vats may be made about the size of a common hogshead, and largest at the bottom.

When hogsheads are procured for dyeing blue on cotton yarn, choose those which are iron bound, and sound in every part. In first preparing a hogshead for dyeing, great care must be taken to stop the bung hole entirely tight, as the indigo dye is of a penetrating nature, and in case it should leak, you would loose the best part of it. In order to secure the bung tight, you will take a square piece of cotton or linen cloth, then rub on some tar and double it about twice, having the tar on the inside, place the cloth on the end of the bung and drive it in firmly, and it will not leak.

When you have taken the head out of your hogshead, you must get a cooper's circular shave to smooth the inside of the upper half of the hogshead, to prevent any injury to the yarn while dipping. The hogshead is then to be washed thoroughly with a broom or brush; then rinsed out well and filled with water to soak for two or three days; then throw out the water, and it will be fit for use.

Before you set your hogshead of blue dye, you will take two pieces of timber or scantling 4 or 5 inches square, each piece being as long as the bottom of the hogshead is in width, then match them together in the middle, by sawing out a gap in each part: this will form a cross for the hogshead to stand on; by this method you can save the dye should it leak.

Yarn Frame.

This frame is used to hang the sticks of yarn across through all the operations, from the boiling of the yarn until it is finished dyeing. It is generally made 8 or 10 feet in length in dye houses, and should be a little narrower than the length of the dye sticks, and about half a foot higher than the length of the cotton skeins.

Observations on grinding Indigo.

There are many different methods practiced in grinding Indigo; we think it not necessary to explain them all, but shall attempt to point out two or three kinds which will be adapted for dyeing blue on a large and small scale.

The mill which we most approve of for grinding Indigo, on a large or moderate scale of blue dyeing, is the tub mill, which is of a simple construction, works easy, and performs the business well and in a short time.

The tub is made of cast iron, and may be about 18 inches in height, 16 inches across the top, and 14½ inches across the bottom on the inside: the bottom must be flat and cast as smooth as possible. On the centre of the bottom must be a step of iron, which should be formed to the kettle when cast. This step should be about one inch and a quarter across and one third of an inch in height, which is for the end of the shaft to run on. The step must be made of a round form with a hollow on the top of it for the shaft to run in.

In the next place 4 cast iron cones will be wanting, the length of which must be such as to run easy between the step and outside of the tub; so that according to the diameter of the bottom of the tub and step, the cones will be 6½ inches in length. The large end of the cones may be about 4 or 4½ inches in diameter and the small end about ½ an inch. The large ends must be a little rounding, so that they will run easy around the side of the tub.

A shaft is to be placed perpendicular in the centre of the tub, the bottom of which is to run on the step.—This must have an iron cross fastened on it near the bottom which is fixed to drive and roll round the cones. These four branches of iron which form the cross must be hardened and may be made nearly half an inch in diameter, and of proper length. These branches must be calculated to strike a little under the centre of the cones so as to drive and roll them in a proper manner.

The shaft may be made of a square bar of iron with the lower end hardened. Towards the upper end you will have a small drum or pully for a belt or strap which can be put in motion by attaching it to other machinery or otherwise.

On the top of the tub a cover must be fixed, formed of two boards with a hole left in the middle for the shaft to run in, which may be made in such a manner as to steady the shaft while turning, or to fix something for that purpose above it. After your tub is cast, you must drill a hole in the bottom of it, one quarter of an inch in diameter, and about two inches from the side; this you will have stopped with a wooden pin while grinding the indigo. When it is ground as fine as oil pour in water to make it quite thin.

The tub must stand firmly on a low bench, so high as to allow a pail to be put under it: in this manner you can draw it off the most conveniently. Observe that the addition of water must not be made until it is ground sufficiently to draw off.

Before you put in the indigo to grind, it must be soaked in water, then broken up so much as not to clog the cones, which are to be placed between the four branches with the small ends next to the step.

It will be found necessary in making the wooden tub and cones for patterns to cast by, that great care should be taken to calculate the length and shape of the cones; which will be first governed by the size and shape of the tub, and the distance between the step and side; and it will be found necessary to try the rolling of the wooden cone before it can be determined whether it is right or not.

In making the tub pattern and cone, it will be well to observe that they must be made of clear white pine stuff and that the staves of the tub may be glued together.

Having known this kind of mill to operate exceedingly well, we have felt a desire that the plan might be generally known among dyers, and have, therefore, been particular to explain the principle and dimensions, in such a manner that any experienced workman might make the pattern. From the circumstance of cones having more surface than round balls, which operate in grinding, it will at once be concluded that the former are the best.

The common indigo mill, which is carried by water, is nothing more than a common iron kettle, that will contain from 3 to 5 pails full; having a perpendicular shaft with an iron cross near the bottom which drives round one, two or more cannon balls.

The common method of grinding indigo by hand is to suspend an iron pot, of a suitable size, with a rope, and using a cannon ball, which is rolled round by taking hold of the legs with the hands. The indigo is first soaked in hot water, then broken up fine and put in the pot a little at a time, with a sufficient quantity of water to prevent the indigo from sticking to the sides and bottom. The ball is then to be rolled round for about one hour; then add some water to make it quite thin, and roll the ball a few times round to mix it; then hold the pot still two or three minutes, and pour off the clear part carefully, into a kettle.

You will then add a little more indigo and water and proceed as before, until it is all ground. In this way you can grind it as fine as oil.

Indigo may be ground fine, for the use of families, with an iron mortar and pestle. First pound all the indigo as fine as coarse gun powder; then put a little indigo in the mortar at a time, and add a little water, but not so much as to occasion it to slop over while stirring round the pestle on the bottom. You will work it round in that manner for about half an hour; then add some water and mix it; then let it stand till it settles, then pour off the clear part; then add a little more indigo, and proceed as before. In this way you can grind it entirely fine.

DIRECTION I.

To Dye Blue on Cotton and Linen in the Cold Dye.

In the first place, fill a hogshead about one quarter full of water.

2. Dissolve 16 pounds copperas in about four pails full of warm water, in a small tub or kettle, and then add it to the water in the hogshead and stir it for two or three minutes, then put 8 pounds of finely ground indigo to it, and rake it up well, for about five minutes.

3. You must now slack 20 pounds of good stone lime with water, which is best done by first putting the lime into a very low or flat tub. When the lime is slacked to a powder, and while it is hot, put it into the hogshead and rake it well several times in the course of two or three hours.

4. The hogshead is then to be filled with water within two inches of the top, then rake it well several times during two days, then leave it to settle over night, and on the morning of the third day, it will be ready for dyeing.

5. If the dye should not be clear, and should not have a deep blue froth or scum on the top, you must add about two pounds of lime, and rake it two or three times during the day, and the next morning it will be fit for use.

6. If the sediment of the dye be of a yellowish green the dye is in a good condition; but if it is of a dull and dark grass green then add about 2 pounds of copperas which you must dissolve in the dye by the help of the dye rake, (the rake is made by putting a handle through a piece of hard board, in the form of one third of a circle, having the rounding edge made thin,) by pounding and raking with it on the bottom of the dye vat. In case the dye should not be clear, add a little lime and it will settle it. If the froth on the surface

of the dye should be of a dull blue color, add some copperas and indigo, which will restore it to a right state for dyeing.

7. When you have dyed two or three days in the dye, you must put into it about 2 pounds of copperas and 3 pounds of lime ; then beat the copperas fine on the bottom with the rake, and stir it up until it is dissolved. After using the dye a few days, should you find that the dye wants more copperas or lime, you may know by attending to the before mentioned rules, how to vary the quantity of the articles which you add; but you will observe, that if the sediment of the dye is of a dark green, it wants copperas, but if it bears too much on the yellow it requires a little lime.

When your dye is ready for dipping, place two narrow strips of wood across the top of the hogshead, to rest your sticks upon, also one to drain the yarn on.

Method of Dyeing.

1. If you calculate to color regularly every day, to perform with advantage, it will be found necessary to boil out enough yarn at once, to last for dyeing at least two days. After you have rinsed the yarn intended to be dyed in one day, you will wring it hard and even a pound at a time, and shake it out well, and place your sticks across the horse, or yarn frame, observing not to shake out the yarn till a few minutes before you begin to color it, as otherwise it would be liable to get dry.

2. To dye blue on cotton, in a profitable manner, there should always be several blue dyes, in a dye house, so that you may have some new dyes, some with about a quarter of the strength used out, some about half and some nearly all used out.

3. Allowing you have several dyes, as above stated, you will begin to dip in the following manner, after stir-

ring in the froth of the dye. Begin by dipping 5 lbs. of yarn in the weakest dye, continually turning one pound after another, for about 10 minutes; then take out one pound after another and place them across the stick to drain. You will then wring it out a little, on a pin, which should be fixed horizontally in a piece of plank over the hogshead; then carry it to the yarn frame and wring it out on the wringing machine, or on the pin which is to be fixed into a post about 3 feet from the floor, having a small tub under it to catch the dye which you wring out.

The yarn is to be shook out on the same pin which you use for wringing; placing the sticks as fast as you wring and shake them out, across the yarn frame.

4. You may dip 20 pounds of white yarn in this manner in the weakest dye. After you have proceeded in this way with each 5 pound parcel, you will then empty the dye which you have wrung out in the tub, back into the hogshead which you have just dipped in. The liquor must be put back again in the same way, in every die that you dip in.

5. You will now observe to take 5 pounds that were dipped last in the weak dye, and dip in the second or next strongest, of which the strength is about half used out. In this manner proceed with the remainder of the 20 pounds, observing always to have that which was dipped last in each of the dyes, dipped first in the next strongest.

6. In the next place, go through with the 20 pounds in the third dye, of which the strength is about one quarter part used out; and lastly give each 5 pounds one more dip in a new dye or the best you have. By this method you will dip 20 pounds of yarn, in 4 dyes of different strength which will finish it, and by observing this rule the yarn will be well penetrated, and of an even color.

7. If your yarn at any time is not like to be deep enough, let it remain in the dye a longer time, but if it

is like to be too dark, then shorter dips must be observed.

After you have finished dyeing for one day, rake up all the dyes, and leave them to settle until next morning. When the weakest dyes are entirely exhausted so they will not stain the yarn, throw them away, rince out the vat and set again. Deep blue yarn is not generally rinsed, but if you wish a bright color you can obtain it by turning your yarn a few minutes in oil of vitriol and water, having it only as sour to the taste as weak vinegar; then wring, rinse, wring again and dry it.

Pale Blue.

When you wish to color yarn pale blue, it must be done by giving it two dips of three minutes each, in a dye half used out, or three dips in a dye still weaker; then wring and air it: afterwards it is to be rinsed, wrung and dryed.

DIRECTION II.

To dye Blue on Cotton and Linen on a small scale suitable for families.

1. Fill a barrel which is well bound, clean and entirely tight, about a quarter part full of water.

2. Dissolve 4 pounds of copperas in a pail of warm water, in a clean kettle, and add it to the water in the barrel: stir it up two or three minutes, then put in two pounds of finely ground indigo of a good quality, and stir it up well for 5 minutes.

3. In the next place you must slack 5 pounds of stone lime, by putting it into a kettle, then sprinkle water on it until it is slacked to powder; while it is yet hot, put it into the barrel, and stir it up well four or five times in the course of two hours; then fill the barrel with

water within two inches of the top; stir it several times during that day and the next, and the morning of the third day it will be in order for dyeing the yarn.

4. Before you begin to dip the yarn, you must fix a small frame, or other convenience, on two sides of the barrel, to rest your dye-sticks across while you are turning the yarn in the dye. This support for the sticks should be about 6 or 8 inches above the top of the barrel, to prevent the ends of the cotton skeins from disturbing the settlings of the dye. Should linen yarn be dyed in a barrel dye, the skeins must be doubled; in that case the sticks are rested on the top of the barrel.

Method of Dyeing.

When your dye is new you can color five pounds the first day which must be well boiled out before hand in weak pearl ash water, or soap suds, then rinsed, wrung and shaken out as described in the first remarks on preparing yarn for dyeing.

1. Place two pounds and a half of yarn on 2 sticks, having the yarn divided into parcels of 3 or 4 skeins, so as to be convenient in wringing it out of the dye; then stir in the froth on the top with a stick. You will then put in the yarn and turn one parcel at a time; continue turning it in the dye for 10 minutes, then wring out one parcel at a time, shake it out well and place it again on the sticks to air.

2. Now take the remainder of the white yarn, being two pounds and a half, and put it on two more sticks, and proceed in the same manner as before. Then wring, shake out and air it, until the green shade changes to blue.

3. It must now be observed, that the yarn which was dipped last, must be dipped first the next time, in order to give both an equal share of the strength of the dye.

You will proceed in this manner until it is dark enough, then wring and dry it.

After you have colored 5 pounds of yarn you will find the dye considerably weaker, so the second day you will dye a less quantity, and repeat the dippings as many times as you find necessary, observing to wring and air between each dipping, as before directed.

When you have colored in your dye two days, it must be recruited a little, by putting in 8 ounces of copperas, which should be pounded a little—also put in three quarters of a pound of slacked lime; then stir it up well for 15 minutes with a rake, which you will find described in direction first. The next morning it will be in order for dyeing.

After you have colored in your dye a few days you will find you cannot finish dark blues; but middling and pale blues can be dyed, which will be wanted for plaids, &c.

When your dye is so much reduced that it will not stain yarn any more, throw it away, wash out the barrel and set again.

DIRECTION III.

Copperas Color on Cotton.

To dye 5 pounds of yarn it will require

1 pound 12 ounces of copperas,
8 pounds of stone lime,
1 ounce sugar of lead,
4 ounces of pearl-ash,
4 ounces of hog's lard.

Use the same proportions to dye any number of pounds.

The yarn must be boiled out a day before hand, but for this color it is not to be rinsed.

Preparation.

1. A day or two before you wish to color your yarn, take a kettle that will contain a pail full, into which you will put six quarts of hot water, then add to it 1 pound 12 ounces of copperas, and 1 ounce of sugar of lead; stir it well until it is all dissolved, and when it is made use of, mix and take off the scum.

2. Another kettle or tub is then to be prepared which will contain half a barrel of water: in this you will put 8 pounds of stone lime, and slack it with water to powder; it is then to be filled up with water and stirred well three or 4 times during the day, then leave it to settle during the night. When it is used, be careful to dip out the clear part only.

3. Now prepare a tub or kettle, which is to be used for dipping the yarn, into which you must put 3 gallons of water, and one gallon of the prepared copperas liquor.

4. Another tub or kettle is to be prepared, into which you will put 6 gallons of clear lime water, and 4 ounces of pearlash. When these two last tubs are prepared, you must then ring and shake out the yarn, and place it on five sticks.

Method of Dyeing.

1. Begin to dip your yarn by putting the 5 pounds at once in the copperas liquor, resting the sticks on the kettle or tub. Turn one pound at a time continually for about 15 minutes; it is then to be taken out, wrung and aired.

2. In the next place dip it in the lime and pearlash liquor, and turn it as before for 10 minutes; then take it out, wring and air it as usual.

3. Now add to the copperas liquor which you have

dipped in, 3 quarts of water, and one quart of the prepared copperas liquor and mix it well together.

4. The lime water which you have dipped in must now be emptied, and 6 gallons of fresh and clear lime water put in.

5. The yarn is now to be dipped in the copperas liquor for 15 minutes, then wrung and aired, then dipped in the lime liquor for 10 minutes: it is then to be aired and rinsed.

6. A tub or kettle is now to be prepared with about 6 gallons of boiling water, then add to it 4 ounces of hog's lard; mix it well and dip the yarn in it for about ten minutes: it is then to be taken out, wrung and dried.

N. B. Should you wish for nothing more than a common copperas color, you may leave out the pearlash and sugar of lead.

Those who wish to dye this or any other color on a larger scale, must use the dyeing articles in the same proportion. The greatest part of the receipts we have given are on a small plan, but it will be found easy to calculate the quantity of liquor and size of the tubs that will be required, to dye cotton yarn in larger quantities.

DIRECTION IV.

Yellow on Cotton.

To dye 2 pounds of yarn it will require the following articles.

8 ounces of allum,
½ an ounce of pearlash,
2 pounds of fustic,
1½ ounces of blue vitriol.

Use the same proportions to dye any number of pounds.

1. The yarn should be boiled out a day before hand,

and after the same method as will be found in the first remarks on preparing yarn for dyeing, it is then to be rinsed, shook out, and put on two sticks.

2. Dissolve in a brass kettle, containing a pail full of hot water, 8 ounces of allum, and half an ounce of pearlash; when the liquor has cooled so you can just endure the hand in it, dip the yarn and turn it continually for about half an hour; it is then to be wrung and shook out; then sink the yarn entirely under the liquor and let it remain over night. The next morning wring it out, and throw away the allum liquor.

Dyeing.

1. Prepare a brass or copper kettle with about three pails of water, and add to it 2 pounds of fustic chips cut up fine, which is to be boiled two hours.

2. The chips are now to be taken out, and the liquor suffered to cool so as to admit the hand in it without scalding; then put in the yarn on the sticks and turn it continually for half an hour: it is then to be taken out, wrung and put on the sticks to air.

3. You must then dissolve one ounce and a half of blue vitriol, a little before hand in some of the warm dye; then add it to the dye liquor: the yarn is then to be dipped and turned in it for about ten minutes, then wring and dry it in the shade.

N. B. Instead of using fustic you may make a strong dye liquor either from yellow oak bark, hickory bark, peach leaves, or arsemart; but should you use either of the barks, the outside of it should be shaved off. After steeping and boiling either of the above, the liquor must either be strained or poured off clear. Should you use peach leaves or arsemart, it will require as much as can be crowded under the water in the kettle.

DIRECTION V.

Yellow on Cotton.

To dye 2 pounds of yarn it will require,
8 ounces of allum,
½ an ounce of pearlash,
1 pound of yellow oak bark,
1 ounce of blue vitriol.

Use the same proportions to dye any number of pounds.

1. Boil out the yarn as usual, then rinse it clean and wring it hard a short time before you dip it.

2. Prepare a brass or copper kettle with a pail full of water, heat it scalding hot, then dissolve in it 8 ounces of allum, and half an ounce of pearlash. When the liquor has cooled a little so that you can turn the yarn without scalding your hand, then place the yarn on two sticks and dip and turn it in the liquor for half an hour: it is then to be taken out, wrung, shook out, and sunk under the liquor to remain over night. The next morning wring it out and nearly dry it. The allum liquor you have used is then to be emptied away.

3. In the next place prepare the brass or copper kettle with about 3 pails full of clean water, and add to it either one pound of yellow oak bark when it is in a green state, or half a pound of it when it is dry. In either case observe to use only the middle and inside coat of the bark. Should you use it dry, cut it up fine or grind it, and then put it loosely into a clean open wove bag.

Whether it is dry or green, you must put it into the water when it is cold; raise the heat by a gentle fire, and when the liquor is blood warm put in theyarn having the sticks rest on the top of the kettle: turn it for one hour and a half, during which time the water should not become warmer than the hand can bear without scalding. You will at last increase the fire and bring the liquor to a scalding heat for a few minutes, then allow it to boil gently for 2 or 3 minutes. It is then to be taken out, cooled, wrung and dried.

DIRECTION VI.

Black on Cotton.

To dye 5 pounds of yarn, it will require
- 2½ pounds of logwood,
- 1½ pounds of sumac,
- ½ peck of stone lime,
- 1 pound 8 ounces copperas,
- 12 ounces of fustic, and
- 4 ounces hog's lard.

Use the same proportions to dye any number of pounds.

The yarn is to be boiled out a day before hand but not rinsed. If you want an excellent black, dye the yarn pale blue first in the indigo dye.

1. A day before you color black, prepare a half barrel tub, into which you will put half a peck of stone lime; slack it with water to a powder, then fill it up with water and stir it two or three times during the day, and the next morning it will be settled clear, and ready for use.

2. Dissolve in a small kettle one pound and a half of copperas, with 6 quarts of warm water, stir it to make it dissolve faster, and when you use it mix it together and skim it.

3. In the next place prepare an iron kettle with about 13 gallons or 5 pails full of water, and add to it two pounds and a half of logwood chips, and one pound and a half of the shoots and leaves of sumac, which must be dried and cut up or ground, then boiled for 2 hours.

4. You must now prepare 3 tubs or kettles, one to be used for the logwood and sumac liquor, one for copperas liquor and one for lime water. Put into the first tub or kettle 8 gallons of clear logwood liquor; in the second about 7 gallons of scalding hot water and 1 gallon of the prepared copperas liquor, and in the third tub or kettle 8 gallons of clear cold lime water, of which you must be careful to use only the clear part, and not disturb the sediment.

Dyeing.

1. Place the yarn on five sticks having a pound on a stick, then dip it in the first tub or kettle, containing the logwood liquor which you prepared first, the liquor being as warm as the hand can be borne in it; then turn the yarn one pound at a time for about half an hour: it is then to be taken out, wrung and aired.

2. In the next place dip it in the second tub or kettle, containing the copperas liqour, in the same manner as before, for about 15 minutes, then wring and air it.

3. Now dip and turn it in the lime water for about five minutes, it is then to be taken out, rinsed and wrung.

4. You must now throw away half of the logwood liquor which you have dipped in, and then put in the remainder of the fresh logwood and sumac liquor, taking only the clear part of it. This liquor should be nearly boiling, so that by adding it to the other it will make the whole of a suitable warmth.

5. Now add to the copperas liquor the remainder of the copperas water, being two quarts that was left.

6. The lime water which you have dipped in must be emptied entirely away; then put in 8 gallons of the clear lime water, as before.

7. Now dip and turn the yarn in the logwood liquor for half an hour; then wring and air it.

8. Next in the copperas liquor for about 15 minutes, then wring and air it.

9. Next in the lime water for 5 minutes then rinse and air it.

10. You will now prepare a kettle and put in about 8 gallons of water, and add to it 12 ounces of fustic chips, boil it for about three quarters of an hour, then pour or strain off the liquor, and when very hot add to it 4 ounces of hog's lard; mix it well together and dip the black yarn for 10 minutes: it is then to be wrung and and dried without rinsing. Should your yarn not be dyed pale blue first, you must dip it 3 different times through the logwood, copperas and lime-water, instead of twice, as has been directed.

N. B. Garments of calico, muslin, cotton stockings, shawls, &c. can be dyed by following the above directions; observing not to have more articles than the liquor of each kind will cover: they must be stirred about in the dye for the same period of time as has been mentioned for yarn.

These kind of cotton articles can also be dyed of any other color which shall be mentioned in the course of dyeing cotton yarn.

DIRECTION VII.

Another Black on Cotton.

For one pound of yarn it will require

- 8 ounces of sumac,
- 6 ounces of copperas,
- $\frac{1}{2}$ an ounce of blue vitriol,
- 8 ounces of logwood,
- 2 ounces of fustic.

Use the same proportions for any number of pounds.

1. Prepare and boil out the yarn a day before hand, as directed in the first remarks on boiling yarn. It is then to be wrung and shaken out; which must be done only a short time before you begin to dip the yarn: it is then to be dyed a pale blue in the indigo dye and then rinsed.

2. Prepare a kettle with about 3 gallons of water, and add to it 8 ounces of dry sumac shoots and leaves which are dry and cut up fine; boil it one hour, adding a little water as the rest boils away: then strain off the liquor into another kettle. When the liquor has cooled so as to admit the hand without scalding, then dip and turn the yarn in it for about half an hour; the yarn is then to be sunk under the liquor to remain over night. The next morning take it out and wring it.

3. In the next place prepare a kettle with about 5 quarts of warm water, dissolve in it 5 ounces of copperas; stir it together, then dip and turn your yarn on a stick for about one hour; it is then to be taken out and wrung; then add to the copperas liquor one ounce more of copperas, and half an ounce of blue vitriol, dissolved in a little hot water before it is added to the copperas liquor, then dip and turn the yarn for about half an hour: it is then to be taken out, rinsed and wrung.

4. Prepare a kettle with about 4 gallons of water, and add to it 8 ounces of logwood chips, and 2 ounces of fustic chips, cut fine, which are to be put in a thin coarse bag and boiled about one hour and a half; then take out the bag, and when the liquor has cooled a little, so that you can just endure the hand in, dip and turn the yarn in it one hour. It is then to be taken out and aired; then rinsed, wrung and dried.

N. B. While speaking of black on cotton it will not be improper to remark that an improvement has been made in dyeing black on linen thread, which is by putting a little tallow or other fresh grease in the hot dye, a little before the yarn is finished, which not only renders the yarn or thread soft, but preserves its strength. As the dyeing of black on linen is so simple and well known, we do not insert the manner of dyeing it. The main point in dyeing a good black on linen, is to have the logwood dye very strong, and plenty of copperas added after all the strength is boiled out of the logwood then dip the thread.

DIRECTION VIII.

To Dye Green on Cotton.

For 2 pounds of yarn it will require
2 pounds 12 ounces of fustic,
6 ounces of logwood,
1 ounce and a half of blue vitriol.

Use the same proportions to dye any number of pounds.

The yarn is to be boiled out a day before hand, then dyed a handsome light pale blue, and rinsed well.

1. Fill a kettle with about 8 gallons of water, add to it 2 pounds and 12 ounces of fustic chips, boil it about 1 hour and a half, adding as much water as what boils away.

2. Boil in another kettle with one gallon of water, 6 ounces of logwood chips for one hour, adding as much water as what boils away; and when you use it take the clear part only.

Dyeing.

1. Prepare a kettle with about 3 gallons of the clear fustic liquor, which must be as warm as the hand will bear. After the yarn is wrung and equally moist, place it on two sticks and dip it in the dye, rest-

ing the sticks on the top of the tub or kettle; turn the yarn continually for about half an hour, then take it out, wring and air it, and throw away the liquor.

2. In the next place put in the same kettle, two and a half gallons of fresh fustic liquor which is clear, and also about 3 quarts of clear logwood liquor, as warm as before mentioned; then dip and turn the yarn as before for about half an hour; it is then to be taken out, wrung and aired, and the liquor emptied away.

3. Now put in the kettle the remainder of the warm and clear fustic liquor, then add to it one ounce and a half of blue vitriol, dissolved in a little warm water before you put it in the dye: then dip and turn the yarn as before for about half an hour: it is then to be taken out and wrung, but not rinsed; then dried in the shade.

Should the color incline too much on the blue shade, use rather less of the logwood liquor, and if it bears too much on the yellow take a little less blue vitriol, and more of the logwood dye.

N. B. Instead of using fustic you may take yellow oak bark or walnut bark. See Direction IV.

DIRECTION IX.

To Dye Red on Cotton.

For 2 pounds of yarn it will require

1 pound 4 ounces of sumac,
8 ounces of allum,
¾ of an ounce of pearlash,
¾ of an ounce of sugar of lead,
3 pounds of nicaragua and
1 table spoonful of compound of aquafortis.

Use the same proportions to dye any number of pounds.

The yarn is to be boiled out a day before hand, then rinsed and wrung.

1. Prepare a brass or copper kettle with about 3 gallons of water, then add to it 1 pound and 4 ounces of sumac, the shoots and leaves being dryed and cut up fine. Boil it for half an hour, then strain off the liquor into a brass, tin or copper kettle; then throw out the sumac, and put the liquor back again.

2. Place your yarn on two sticks, being previously shook out, and when the liquor has cooled so that you can just endure the hand in it, dip and turn the yarn for half an hour; it is then to be wrung out and put in again, sinking it entirely under the liquor, and let it remain over night. Next morning it is to be taken out wrung and dried in the shade.

3. In the next place, prepare a brass, tin, or copper kettle with about 3 gallons of hot water, then dissolve in it 8 ounces of allum, three quarters of an ounce of pearlash, and three quarters of an ounce of sugar of lead. When it is entirely dissolved and the liquor cooled so that you can bear the hand in it, enter your yarn on the sticks, and turn it for about half an hour: it is then to be sunk entirely under the liquor, to remain over night. The next morning take it out, rince lightly and wring it.

Dyeing.

1. Prepare a brass or copper kettle with about 10 gallons of water, add to it 3 pounds of nicaragua chips. Boil for about one hour and a half, then let the chips settle at the bottom—about two and a half gallons of the clear liquor is now to be taken out and put in another clean brass or copper kettle.

2. Now place your yarn on the sticks, and when the dye is warm as you can endure the hand in it, then

dip and turn the yarn in it for about half an hour; it is then to be taken out and wrung, and the liquor emptied away.

3. About two and a half gallons more of the fresh and clear dye liquor is now to be put in the kettle, being as warm as before directed; then dip and turn the yarn in it for about half an hour, then wring it out.

4. You must now empty half of the liquor away which has just been used, then put in some fresh scalding hot dye liquor, to make as much of the whole as you had before, and of the same warmth at the time of dipping. The yarn is now to be dipped and turned again as before, for about half an hour; it is then to be taken out and wrung.

The yarn at this time will probably be of a dark red color, but if not, empty out half of the liquor and fill up with clear hot dye liquor as before; then dip again, wring, and empty away the liquor.

5. The kettle is now to be rinsed, then put in about 3 gallons of clear water, which is not to be made warm; then add to it a table spoonful of the compound of aqua fortis. When you have mixed the compound well with the water, one of the colored skeins is to be dipped in it for 3 or 4 minutes; should it produce a bright red color, you may put in all your yarn for about 10 minutes, then wring it out. Should the skein which you tried not have changed its appearance, in that case you will add a trifle more of the compound until the color is effected to your wishes.

6. Now put in your tub or kettle, about 2½ gallons of nicaragua liquor as warm as has been before directed, then dip and turn the yarn in it for about half an hour. It is then to be wrung and dried without rinsing.

Method of making the Compound of Aqua-Fortis.

Take a junk or glass bottle and put in it 4 ounces of aqua-fortis and as much rain or soft river water—when you have mixed it together add to it ¼ of an ounce of salamoniac, pounded fine, then mix it well together: after which, is also to be added, ½ an ounce of grained tin, which is conducted in the following manner.

First melt the block tin over a fire, then pour it a distance from above, of about 4 or 5 feet, gradually into a bason of cold water: by this means you will find the tin formed into light and fine pieces, and is then ready for dissolving in the aqua-fortis. You will then put one piece into the bottle at a time, letting one piece dissolve before another is added. When it is all dissolved, let it stand for a day or two. After that space of time the liquor will be clear, of an amber color, and fit for use. Keep the bottle well stopped, with a wax or glass stopper, and it will keep good several months. When you use it, take the clear part only.

DIRECTION X.

Orange color on Cotton.

To dye 5 pounds of yarn it will require
4 ounces of Anatto or Otter, and
8 ounces of Pearlash.

Use the same proportions to dye any number of pounds.

The yarn is to be boiled out before hand as usual, and wrung, but not not rinsed.

1. Prepare a brass or copper kettle with about eight gallons of clean water, then add to it eight ounces of anatto which must be cut up fine, and eight ounces of pearlash; boil it for one hour, then put the liquor into a clean tub or kettle to settle a few hours or until you want it for use.

2. Take about 6 gallons of the clear anatto liquor, put it in a brass kettle and heat it scalding hot by keeping it at the side of a fire, then place your yarn on five

sticks, and dip and turn it for twenty minutes; it is then to be taken out and wrung.

3. In the next place add about half a gallon of fresh clear anatto liquor to the rest in the kettle, keeping the dye nearly scalding hot; then dip and turn the yarn for about twenty minutes; it is then to be taken out and wrung, then rinced, wrung, and dried in the shade.

N. B. In dyeing orange, roco is often used instead of anatto as it comes at a much less price. If you choose to make use of roco, you must take about double the quantity, that is, for five pounds of yarn it will require eight ounces of roco, and ten ounces of pearlash.

DIRECTION XI.

To Dye Madder Red on Cotton.

For 2 pounds of yarn it will require

1 pound 4 ounces of sumac,
8 ounces of pearlash,
3 ounces of stone lime,
8 ounces of allum,
¾ of an ounce of salamoniac,
2 ounces of hog's lard,
2 pounds of madder,
2 ounces of chalk,
1 pound 8 ounces of wheat bran,
3 ounces of hard soap.

Use the same proportions to dye any number of pounds.

The yarn is to be boiled out before hand, then rinsed and wrung.

First prepare a brass or copper kettle with 3 gallons of clean water, then add to it one pound four ounces of dried sumac, (the shoots and leaves being cut up fine together,) boil it for about half an hour, and strain off the clear part into a clean tub or brass kettle. When the liquor has cooled so you can bear the hand in it, place the yarn upon two sticks, snd dip and turn it for about half an hour; the yarn is then to be sunk under the liquor, to remain over night: next morning it is to be taken out, wrung, and dryed in the shade.

2. In the next place prepare a kettle with about one gallon and a half of hot water, then dissolve in it eight ounces of pearlash, and add three ounces of slacked lime; stir it well together and let it settle for two hours.

3. Now place a kettle over a fire with about one gallon of water; when it has arrived at a scalding heat, add 8 ounces of allum, and the clear part of the lime and pearlash liquor—also add to it $\frac{3}{4}$ of an ounce of salamoniac, (which is pounded and dissolved in a little hot water before hand) then mix them all together, and while the liquor is still quite hot, then also add 2 ounces of lard, and mix the whole well together.

4. The yarn is then to be placed on the sticks, and when the liquor has cooled so the hand can be borne in it, then dip and turn the yarn about half an hour; it is then to be taken out, wrung, and dried in the shade, then rinsed well and again dried.

5. Heat the same liquor again, and dip and turn the yarn for about half an hour; it is then to be wrung and dried in the shade, then rinsed, wrung, shook out, and put on the sticks.

Dyeing.

1. Prepare a brass or copper kettle with about ten gallons of clean soft water, then add to it, when the water is cold, two pounds of madder broken up fine, and two ounces of pounded chalk. In dyeing on this small scale, it will be found necessary to place the kettle at the side of a fire, to allow you to turn the yarn on the sticks.

2. You will now place the yarn on the sticks, and when the madder liquor is of a blood warmth, put in the yarn and turn it constantly, having the heat of the dye increase moderately by keeping only a gentle fire. When the dye has become so warm as you can just endure the hand in it, then allow it to get no hotter for two hours, turning the yarn during that time. You will then increase the heat to a scald for five minutes, having a pail of cold water standing by to dip your hands in often, while turning the yarn; it is then to be taken out, cooled, and rinsed.

3. Now rinse the kettle, put in about ten gallons of water, and add to it two quarts of wheat bran in a clean bag, and two ounces of hard soap cut up in thin pieces. Bring the liquor to a boil, then put in the yarn and let it boil for half an hour; it is then to be taken out, cooled, and rinsed, then wrung, and dried in the shade.

DIRECTION XII.

Madder Red on Cotton, as practiced in France.

To dye one pound of yarn it will require

10 ounces of sumac,
4 ounces of allum,
1 pound of madder,
2 ounces of pearlash,
1 ounce of lime and,
12 ounces of wheat bran.

Use the same proportions to dye any number of pounds.

1. Prepare and boil out your yarn the day before you color, and in the same manner, as you will find stated in the first remarks. It is afterwards to be rinsed, wrung, and shaken out, a short time before you begin to dip the yarn.

2. In the next place prepare a brass or copper kettle with about two and a half gallons of water; then add

to it, 10 ounces of sumac leaves and shoots, which should be cut in the month of August or September, and then dryed and cut up fine before used. Boil it for about half an hour, then strain the clear liquor off, throw away the sumac and put the liquor back again.

3. When the liquor has cooled, to a little less than a scalding heat; then place the yarn on a stick and dip and turn it about half an hour; then sink it entirely under the liquor, and let it remain over night. Next morning wring it out moderately, and dry it; then empty away the liquor.

4. Prepare the kettle with about 5 quarts of hot water and dissolve in it 4 ounces of allum; then dip and turn the yarn as before, for about half an hour; then sink it entirely under the liquor and let it remain over night. Next morning wring it moderately and dry it.

Dyeing.

1. Prepare a brass or copper kettle, with about five or six gallons of water; then add to it 8 ounces of good madder, broken up fine. When the liquor has become a little more than blood warm, place the yarn on a stick, then turn it continually for one hour, keeping the liquor the whole time no warmer than you can bear the hand in it. The last part of the time, allow it to be towards scalding hot; the yarn is then to be taken out, wrung and aired.

2. In the next place, dissolve 2 ounces of pearlash in a pint of water, and add to it half a pint of clear lime water, made from about an ounce of slacked stone lime, which is to be mixed before hand in cold water, and then left to settle clear. Now put the above mixture of pearlash and clear lime water into the madder dye and stir it well together. When the madder dye is at a little less than a scalding heat, enter the yarn by sinking it entirely under the liquor, and bring it to boil for 5 minutes; it is then to be taken out and cooled; then rinsed and wrung.

3. The madder dye is now to be emptied away; then put in about 5 gallons of water, and add 8 ounces more of madder, broken up fine. You will then proceed in the same manner and time as before; but without adding any pearlash or lime water, observing to keep the dye something less than a scalding heat, for 1 hour, turning the yarn continually during that time. It is then to be taken out and wrung, then throw away the dye.

4. To brighten the color, prepare the kettle with about 5 gallons of water and put into it 12 ounces of wheat bran (previously put into a clean bag) and one ounce of hard soap cut up fine and dissolved. Bring the water to a boil, then enter the yarn and boil it for half an hour. It is then to be taken out, cooled and rinsed; then wrung and dried in the shade.

DIRECTION XIII.

To Dye Purple on Cotton.

For 2 pounds of yarn, it will require

1 pound 4 ounces of sumac,
1 pound 4 ounces of logwood,
1 ounce of allum,
$\frac{1}{4}$ of an ounce of verdigris.

Use the same proportions to dye any number of pounds.

1. Boil out the yarn the day before hand as usual, and after the same method, as you will find directed in the first remarks. Afterwards it is to be wrung, shook out and put on sticks, a short time before you dip the yarn.

2. In the next place prepare an iron, brass or copper kettle, with about 4 gallons of water; then add to it 1 pound 4 ounces of sumac shoots and leaves cut up fine; which is to boil for about half an hour; then strain off

the liquor, throw away the sumac and put the liquor back again.

3. When the liquor has cooled to a little less than a scalding heat, dip your yarn and turn it on the sticks for about half an hour; then sink it entirely under the liquor and let it remain over night. Next morning it is to be taken out and wrung, then empty away the liquor.

4. Now prepare a kettle with about 7 gallons of water; then add to it 1 pound and 4 ounces of logwood chips, which is to be boiled for about one hour: then let it stop boiling, and allow the chips to settle at the bottom.

5. Three gallons of the clear logwood liquor is now to be put into another kettle, and when the liquor has cooled so as to admit the hand without scalding, place the yarn on two sticks and dip and turn it for about 20 minutes: it is then to be taken out, wrung and aired.

6. Take about a pint of hot water and dissolve in it two thirds of the allum mentioned at first; also one quarter of an ounce of pounded verdigris. When it is entirely dissolved, pour it into the logwood liquor, which you dipped in last; then mix it together and dip and turn the yarn again as before, for about 20 minutes; it is then to be taken out wrung and aired.

7. Now add 2 or 3 quarts of very hot logwood liquor, taken out clear from the other kettle; then dip and turn the yarn again for 20 minutes; then wring it out and empty away the liquor.

8. Put into your kettle the remainder of the logwood liquor, which must be as warm as the hand can bear, while dipping the yarn: in this liquor dissolve the remainder of the allum, being one third of an ounce; then dip and turn the yarn as before for about 20 minutes; it is then to be taken out, wrung and dried.

DIRECTION XIV.

Drab Color on Cotton.

To dye 5 pounds of yarn, it will require
10 ounces of allum,
10 ounces of copperas,
10 ounces of fustic,
10 ounces of sumac.

Use the same proportions to dye any number of pounds.

1. Boil out the yarn a day before you wish to color, and in the same manner as pointed out in the remarks on preparing and boiling : it is to be rinsed and wrung a short time before you dip it.

2. Prepare an iron, brass or copper kettle, with about 6 gallons of water ; bring it nearly to a scalding heat ; then dissolve 10 ounces of allum and 10 ounces of copperas, in about 1 gallon and a half of hot water, and add it to the water in the kettle, and mix it well.

3. Place your yarn on 5 sticks, and when the liquor is as warm as you bear the hand in it, dip and turn the yarn for about half an hour : it is then to be taken out and wrung.

4. The liquor which you have used is now to be emptied away ; then prepare the kettle with about 8 gallons of water, add to it 10 ounces of fustic chips, and ten ounces of sumac shoots and leaves, which are to be dryed and cut up fine. Both of these articles are to be put into a thin coarse bag and boiled for about three quarters of an hour ; otherwise you can boil the fustic and sumac without putting them in a bag, but in that case you must strain the liquor.

5. When the liquor has cooled, so that you can just endure the hand in it, then dip and turn the yarn on the sticks for half an hour. It is then to be wrung out and dried without rinsing.

You can give it different shades, by adding more or

less fustic and sumac: or by adding a small proportion of logwood liquor.

DIRECTION XV.

To Dye a Reddish Brown on Cotton.

For 5 pounds of yarn it will require
2 pounds 8 ounces of fustic,
1 pound of nicaragua,
1 pound of logwood,
8 ounces of copperas,
$\frac{1}{4}$ of a gill of aqua fortis compound.

Use the same proportions to dye any number pounds.

1. Boil out the yarn the day before you wish to color, in the same manner as directed in the first remarks on boiling yarn: it is then to be wrung out a short time before you begin to dip the yarn.

2. Prepare an iron, brass or copper kettle, with about 8 gallons of water: then add to it 2 pounds 8 ounces of fustic chips, put in a thin coarse bag; and boiled for about three quarters of an hour. You can boil the fustic loose in the kettle if you wish; but in that case, the liquor must be strained or taken off clear before you dip the yarn in it.

3. In the next place, dissolve eight ounces of copperas in about one gallon of warm water, and add it to the fustic liquor: then stir it well together and suffer the liquor to cool a little, so that you can just endure the hand in it while dipping.

4. Place the yarn on 5 sticks, then dip and turn it for about half an hour. It is then to be wrung out and the liquor emptied away.

5. Prepare the kettle with about 8 gallons of water, then add to it 1 pound of nicaragua, and 1 pound of logwood, both chipped and put into a thin coarse bag and boiled about three quarters of an hour. Now

take the bag out, and add to the liquor a quarter of a gill of aqua fortis compound: then stir the whole well together, and suffer the liquor to cool a little, so that the hand can just be endured in it while dipping.

6. Dip and turn the yarn again for about fifteen minutes: it is then to be taken out, rinsed, wrung and dried.

DIRECTION XVI.

To Dye Logwood Blue on Cotton.

For 5 pounds of yarn it will require
6 ounces of blue vitriol,
2 pounds 8 ounces of logwood.
Use the same proportions for any number of pounds.

1. Boil out the yarn a day previous to coloring, and in the same manner as pointed out in the remarks on boiling yarn; after which it must be wrung, a short time before you dip it.

2. Prepare an iron, brass or copper kettle with about eight gallons of water, bring it nearly to a scalding heat, then dissolve in it six ounces of blue vitriol.

3. Place the yarn on five sticks, then dip and turn it for about one hour: it is then to be taken out and wrung, and the liquor which you have just dipped in is to be emptied away.

4. Prepare the kettle with about 8 gallons of water, and add to it, two pounds eight ounces of logwood chips, which is to be put in a thin coarse bag and boiled for about three quarters of an hour; then take out the bag and let the liquor cool so that the hand may be borne in it; then dip and turn the yarn in it for about half an hour. It is then to be taken out and wrung.

5. In the next place, dissolve in the liquor you have just dipped in, 2 ounces of pearlash; then dip and turn the yarn again for 20 minutes. It is then to be

taken out and wrung. Should you wish the color darker, add one ounce of blue vitriol to the liquor ; and when dissolved, dip again for 10 minutes. It is then to be wrung and dried without rinsing.

DIRECTION XVII.

Olive Color on Cotton.

To dye 2 pounds of yarn it will require
8 ounces of fustic,
6 ounces of pearlash,
2 ounces of logwood,
½ an ounce of verdigris.

Use the same proportions to dye any number of pounds.

1. Boil out the yarn a day before hand, and after the same manner as you will find stated in the remarks on preparing and boiling yarn. It is then to be wrung a short time before you commence dipping.

2. Prepare an iron, brass or copper kettle, with about 3 gallons of water, add to it eight ounces of fustic chips, put it in a thin coarse bag, boil it for about three quarters of an hour; you will then dissolve in the hot liquor 6 ounces of pearlash : also add to it, two quarts of clear logwood liquor, made from 2 ounces of logwood. Then add half an ounce of verdigris, pounded fine, which must be well dissolved before hand in a small quantity of the logwood liquor ; then stir the whole well together.

Dyeing.

1. When the liquor has cooled, so you can bear the hand in it, place your yarn on 2 sticks, and dip and turn it in the dye for about half an hour, then wring and air it.

2. Should you wish the color darker, then add a little more logwood liquor to the rest, then dip and turn

the yarn again for about fifteen minutes, it is then to be wrung out and aired. For a very dark olive, you will prepare a kettle with a suitable quantity of water, and add to it three ounces of copperas, dissolved before hand in a little water, then enter your yarn and turn it for about 4 or 5 minutes; it is then to be rinsed, wrung and dipped again in the fustic and logwood liquor for 10 minutes ;then rinsed, wrung and dried.

DIRECTION XVIII.

Olive on Cotton, with a Blue Ground.

To dye 2 pounds of yarn it will require
8 ounces of sumac,
3 ounces of copperas,
8 ounces of fustic,
½ an ounce of verdigris,
1 ounce and a half of blue vitriol.

Use the same proportions to dye any number of pounds.

1. Boil out the yarn and afterwards dye it a light blue in the indigo dye; it is then to be rinsed, and wrung a short time before dipping.

2. Prepare an iron, brass or copper kettle, with about 3 gallons of water; then add to it 8 ounces of sumac shoots and leaves cut up fine. Boil it for three quarters of an hour, then strain the liquor or pour off the clear part, and suffer it to cool so that you can endure the hand in it while dipping.

3. Place the yarn on two sticks, and dip and turn it for about half an hour; then sink the yarn entirely under the liquor and let it remain over night; next morning it is to be taken out and wrung: then empty away the liquor.

4. Prepare the kettle with about 3 gallons of water, then dissolve in it 2 ounces of copperas; you will then

dip and turn the yarn in it for about 15 minutes ; it is then to be rinsed and wrung.

5. In the next place, empty away the copperas liquor and put in the kettle about 3 gallons of water; then add 8 ounces of fustic chips, which are to be put in a thin coarse bag and boiled three quarters of an hour; you will then take out the bag and add half an ounce of verdigris, pounded fine and dissolved in a little of the hot fustic liquor before hand, then stir the whole well together.

When the liquor has cooled so that the hand can be borne in it; then dip and turn the yarn in the dye for about half an hour. It is then to be taken out and wrung.

6. Add to the liquor which you have just dipped in one ounce and a half of blue vitriol, which must be pounded and dissolved in a little of the hot liquor before hand, then dip and turn your yarn for 10 minutes. Should you not find the color dark enough, add some logwood liquor and copperas to the remaining liquor ; then dip and turn again for about ten minutes; and rinse, wring and dry it.

DIRECTION XIX.

Cinnamon Color on Cotton.

To dye 1 pound of yarn it will require
4 ounces of allum,
½ an ounce of blue vitriol,
8 ounces of fustic,
4 ounces of sumac,
8 ounces of madder.

Use the same proportions to dye any number of pounds.

1. Boil out the yarn a day before coloring it, and after the manner you will find directed in the remarks on boiling, it is then to be rinsed and wrung.

2. Prepare a kettle with about 6 quarts of water, and dissolve in it 2 ounces of allum and half an ounce of blue vitriol; heat the water as warm as the hand will bear, then place the yarn on a stick and dip and turn it in the liquor for about half an hour: it is then to be taken out and wrung.

3. In the next place, add 8 ounces of fustic chips to the allum liquor. The fustic chips are to be put in a bag and boiled for about one hour, in the mean time adding about 2 quarts of water.

The bag is then to be taken out, and the liquor suffered to cool to a little less than a scalding heat; then dip and turn the yarn for about one hour: it is then to be wrung out and aired. Add to the liquor you have last dipped in, 2 ounces of allum, (dissolved in a little hot water before hand) the yarn is to be dipped and turned in the liquor again for half an hour; next wrung out and aired.

4. Prepare a brass or copper kettle with about 5 gallons of clear water, then add to it 8 ounces of madder, broken up fine, and 4 ounces of the shoots and leaves of sumac, which last must be cut up fine and put into a thin coarse bag; heat the liquor slowly over a moderate fire; when it is little more than blood warm put your yarn on a stick and dip and turn it for 1 hour: during which time the dye must be at a little less than a scalding heat. The yarn is now to be taken out, wrung and aired.

Should you wish to brighten the color, you will next rinse out the kettle and put in as much water as will cover the yarn; then add to it one ounce of soap, cut up fine; bring the liquor to boil, then enter the yarn under the liquor and boil it about half an hour; it is then to be taken out, cooled, rinsed, wrung and dried.

DIRECTION XX.

Brown on Cotton.

To dye 5 pounds of yarn it will require
2 pounds 8 ounces of fustic,
2 pounds of logwood,
4 ounces of blue vitriol,
8 ounces of copperas.

Use the same proportions to dye any number of pounds.

1. Boil out the yarn a day previous to coloring, and after the manner directed in the first remarks on boiling. Afterwards it is to be rinsed and wrung a short time before you commence coloring it.

2. Prepare a kettle with about 8 gallons of water, and add to it 2 pounds 8 ounces of fustic chips, which are to be put into a thin coarse bag and boiled about 1 hour. Take out the bag and add to the liquor 8 ounces of copperas, (dissolved before hand in about a gallon of warm water,) stir it well together, and when the liquor has cooled so as to allow the hand to be borne in it is ready for dipping.

3. Place the yarn on 5 sticks and dip and turn it half an hour: then take it out, wring it and empty away the liquor which you have just used.

4. Prepare the kettle again with about 8 gallons of water, and add to it 2 pounds of logwood chips put into a coarse bag and boil it about three quarters of an hour ; then take out the bag and dissolve in the liquor 4 ounces of blue vitriol. Allow the liquor to cool so much that you can endure the hand in it without scalding : then place the yarn on sticks and dip and turn it for half an hour : it is then to be wrung out, rinsed and dried.

DIRECTION XXI.

Slate Color on Cotton.

For 2 pounds of yarn it will require
5 ounces of copperas, and
1 pound of sumac.

Use the same proportions to dye any number of pounds.

1. Boil out the yarn a day before coloring it, and in the same manner as directed in the first remarks on preparing yarn for dyeing. It is to be wrung out a short time before you begin dipping it.

2. Prepare a kettle with about 3 gallons of warm water; add to it 5 ounces of copperas and when it is perfectly dissolved place your yarn on 2 sticks, then dip and turn it in the liquor for about half an hour: it is then to be taken out and wrung.

3. In the next place prepare another kettle with about 3 gallons of water, and add to it 1 pound of the shoots and leaves of sumac, dried and cut up fine.—Boil it for about half an hour, then strain off the clear part of the liquor, throw away the sumac, and pour it back again into the kettle.

4. After the liquor has cooled so that you can bear the hand in it, then place the yarn on the sticks, and dip and turn it for about half an hour; then wring it out and air it. If the color is not dark as you wish, dip again in the copperas liquor for 10 minutes, then lastly, in the sumac liquor for 15 minutes; then wring and dry without rinsing.

DIRECTION XXII.

Slate Color on Cotton.

To dye 2 pounds of yarn it will require
3 ounces of nutgalls,

½ an ounce of allum,
3 ounces of copperas,
6 ounces of logwood.

Use the same proportions to dye any number of pounds.

1. Boil out the yarn the day before coloring it, and in the same manner as directed in the first remarks on preparing yarn for dyeing. After it is boiled, rinse and wring it out a short time before you commence dipping.

2. Prepare a kettle with about three gallons of water, and add to it 3 ounces of nutgalls, pounded fine; boil for half an hour, then let the galls settle at the bottom and take the clear part of the liquor off into another kettle or tub: otherwise you may strain it.

3. When the liquor has cooled so that you can bear the hand in it; place the yarn on the sticks and dip and turn it in the liquor for about half an hour: it is then to be taken out and wrung.

4. Empty away the gall liquor and prepare the kettle with about 3 gallons of water; then add to it 6 ounces of logwood chips, which are to be put into a bag and boiled about ¾ of an hour, then take out the bag and add half an ounce of allum. When the allum is entirely dissolved, and the liquor cooled so that you can endure the hand in it, dip and turn the yarn for 20 minutes. It is then to be wrung out and aired, and the allum liquor emptied away.

5. Next put about 2 gallons of cold water into the kettle, and dissolve in it 3 ounces of copperas; then dip and turn the yarn in the liquor for 10 minutes; then rinse, wring and dry it.

DIRECTION XXIII.

Brown on Cotton.

To dye 5 pounds of yarn it will require
4 ounces of pearlash,

1 pound of copperas,
1 bushel of maple or white oak bark.

Use the same proportions to dye any number of pounds.

1. Boil out the yarn a day before coloring, as usual.

2. Prepare a kettle with about 8 gallons of water, bring it nearly to a scalding heat, then add 4 ounces of pearlash. When it is dissolved, place your yarn on 5 sticks and dip and turn it in the liquor for half an hour. It is then to be taken out and wrung, and the pearlash liquor emptied out.

3. In the next place, prepare a kettle with about 5 or 6 pails of water, and put in 1 bushel of maple bark, or instead, take the same quantity of white oak bark.—Boil it 2 hours, adding a little water occasionally; then take out the bark and strain the liquor.

4. When the liquor is about scalding hot, add one pound of copperas, and stir it round until it is all dissolved. You will now suffer the liquor to cool a little, then dip and turn the yarn on the sticks for about 15 minutes: it is then to be wrung out and aired. Dip and turn again for 15 minutes, and then wring it out: so proceed for 1 hour. It is then to be rinsed, wrung and dried.

Scouring Woollen Cloth from the Loom.

Flannel is generally wove in the grease in factories, which method is preferred to scouring the yarn before weaving; not only from its being more convenient, but it has a tendency to produce closer cloth and is less liable to break than yarn wove in a dry state.

When the cloth is wove and taken from the loom, it should be carefully and thoroughly trimmed, by taking from it all the knots, double threads and loose ends; it is then ready for scouring, which is done in the following manner, viz: For a stock of cloth of 60 pounds weight, or 70 yards of flannel 1 yard wide, take 6 gallons of old urine and 6 gallons of soft soap; mix them well together in 6 gallons of hot water: when the liquor is as warm as you can bear the hand in it, spread the flannel on the floor, and wet it equally; then enter the cloth in the fulling mill, and let it operate about fifteen minutes. It is then to be taken out and laid open, to discover if any parts are dry; if so, wet those places with the same kind of liquor as before. The cloth is now to be laid in the mill again, which should run nearly half an hour; you may then discover whether the grease is sufficiently raised, by wringing a small place in the cloth very hard: should the grease come out easy and free, it is scoured enough. You will then pour into the mill slowly, 4 or 5 pails full of warm water, and after it has produced a lather, then admit cold water to run through it for a few minutes, or until the filth and grease is well washed out. Should the cloth turn irregularly, handle it over and put it in the mill again until it is rinsed clean. It must then be taken out and dryed for the next process or fulling.

It will not be improper to observe that the mill with fallers will start the grease better than the crank mill, but the latter is the best for washing; on the whole, the crank mill is to be preferred where only one is used for both purposes.

It is of the utmost importance that cloth should be entirely cleansed from grease; for should any remain, it would prevent its receiving and retaining a bright and permanent color; besides such cloths always crock, and will not admit of being finished in a workman-like manner.

Another Method to Scour Woollen Cloth from the Loom.

To 1 barrel of urine add 1 bushel of hog dung, mix it well, then use enough of the clear liquor to wet the cloth. After it is equally wet let it run in the mill for five minutes, then take it out, handle it over, and afterwards pack it together in a warm place until it heats through; then lay it in the mill and put on a pail full of urine, let it run 10 minutes, then take it out and handle it until cool. You will then lay it in again and permit cold water to run through it for half an hour, handling once in that time—then dry it for fulling.

Fulling.—This branch of business, like other arts, requires a strict attention to succeed well.

For a stock of cloth of about 60 pounds weight, or 70 yards of yard wide flannel, take 5 pounds of hard soap, that is free from rosin, shave it fine and put it into a kettle with 6 gallons of soft water: place it over a gentle fire and stir it until the soap is dissolved: afterwards suffer it to cool down to blood warmth. You will then take nearly half of the liquor and wet the cloth evenly, enter it in the mill and let it run about one hour. It is then to be taken out and overhauled; lay it in the mill again and add the soap liquor as often as it inclines to get dry, but observe not to get it very wet, as that would tend to stop the felting of the cloth.

Should the cloth full rather slow, handle it over once in about an hour and a half—adding liquor occasionally; proceed in this manner until the cloth has become of a suitable thickness, or the width that is wanted.

Now wet the cloth with 4 or 5 pails of warm water, let it work a few minutes, then admit cold water until it runs off clear: it is then to be taken out and stretched on the pin smooth, at which time it will be ready for napping, &c.

Of scouring dyed cloth.—For a stock of cloth, 60 pounds weight, or about 70 yards of narrow cloth, it will require 3 gallons of soft soap, 4 gallons of urine and 4 gallons of soft water: put them into a kettle and heat scalding hot: stir it together until dissolved, then suffer it to cool down to a blood warmth. Wet the cloth evenly, and enter it in the fulling mill to work for half an hour, then take it out and overhaul it; lay it in the mill again and let it run until the superfluous coloring matter is raised, then admit it to be washed in the mill with water until clean.

N. B. Observe that the cloth should be rinsed in the mill with water only after it is dyed, then dryed before you proceed to scour as last directed.

Of Blue on Woollen.—Wool and woollen stuffs of all kinds, are dyed blue without any other preparation than wetting them well in luke-warm water, squeezing them well afterwards, or letting them drain. This precaution is necessary that the color may the more easily insinuate itself into the body of the wool, that it may be equally dispersed throughout; nor is this to be omitted in any kind of colors, whether the subject be wool or cloth.

As to wool in the fleece, which is used in manufacturing cloth for mixtures, or intended for only one color, and which it is necessary to dye before it is spun, it is first prepared in another manner, viz: it is scoured, and thereby divested of the natural fat it had when on the body of the animal. As this operation is properly the dyer's, and is indispensable in wool which is to be dyed before it is spun, let the color be what it will, we have given the best process for scouring it—see "observations on scouring wool."

DIRECTION XXIV.

Method of Setting and Working the Indigo Vat.

There are several methods of erecting the indigo vat: some are constructed on the plan of heating the dye while in the vat, while others are calculated only for working the dye, and depend on heating it in a copper near by. Having seen vats worked of both descriptions, we think the former is to be preferred, particularly from its convenience in keeping the dye at regular heat, as also saving much time and trouble in emptying it backwards and forwards from the vat and copper, which is not only a means of wasting the liquor, but is in some degree injurious to the dye, by exposing it greatly to the action of air, which it will be perceived has an affect to blacken it.

The most approved method of erecting vats, that are calculated for heating the blue dye while therein, and securing a regular heat while dyeing wool or cloth, is the following. Have the bottom or lower part of a vat formed with a cast iron kettle, having it of such a size as the extent of your work requires. The staves which are to form the chief part of the vat, should be made of pine plank, thoroughly seasoned, clear stuff, about 2 inches thick, and well bound with iron hoops. The vat should be largest at the top, and the bottom part calculated of such a size as will set 3 or 4 inches in depth, on the inside from the top of the kettle, allowing a sufficient space to cork it thoroughly with oakum between the top of the kettle and staves. Previous to this, an iron hoop must be fastened round the top of the kettle, to render it secure. After the vat is thus prepared, place it in a convenient spot, with the bottom of the kettle set a few inches in the ground; then surround it with brick work to a suitable height, having a small fireplace in front, and a flue against the kettle, made in a circular form to convey the heat to all sides of the dye, and then made to pass into a chimney.

To set a vat of 6 barrels, you will first fill the vat about half full of boiling water. Then 1½ pounds potash previously dissolved in hot water, is to be added—then take 12 quarts of wheat bran that is free from flour and sprinkle into the vat; 12 ounces of good madder is next to be added, which should be broken fine; the whole is then to be well mixed together by stirring it with the rake. In the next place pour into the vat $1\frac{1}{2}$ pounds of best indigo, that has been ground in water as fine as oil, rake it well a few minutes, then cover the vat close, observing through all this process the vat should be closely covered, except at the time of introducing the different articles.

In setting a new vat the evening is the best time, having all the materials added by ten at night. The morning after setting, a gentle fire is to be made, to enable the dyer to keep up a moderate heat in the vat, but observe not to allow the dye to become hardly scalding hot: at this time the vat is to be opened and plunged with the rake from the top to the bottom, which will cause bubbles to appear. If on repeating the plunges a few times, a thick deep blue froth arises on the surface of the dye, and remains floating, the liquor wearing the appearance of a dark green, the dye may be pronounced to be in a good state. Should it be found necessary to rake and plunge the dye 2 or 3 times, you will observe to cover the vat close and let it remain an hour between each trial of plunging.

Should your vat be set without any convenience attached to it for heating, and thereby suffered to become cool before it has come to work, there will be no head arise on the surface, although it may otherwise be good. In this case you will have to reheat the dye in the copper, and then pour it back again into the vat; this will retard business and cause trouble, whereas the vat that has a kettle for its bottom, can be kept at a regular heat with the greatest ease.

If the dye, on opening it the morning after setting, has a pale blue appearance, nearly half a pound of fine madder is to be sprinkled into it. Should the liquor have a whitish scum, it is a proof that it does not work, and will not color in that state: in this case a part of the dye should be reheated, and a small quantity of all its ingredients added and in the same proportion as at first. A handful of lime slacked to powder should then be put into warm water: after it has settled, pour the clear part into the vat, rake it well and allow it to stand an hour between each raking, observing not to uncover the vat often, but let the air be excluded as much as possible by surrounding the top with cloths or blankets, securing the heat to that degree that you can just endure your hand in a few seconds. When the dye has come to a head and is in a good state for dyeing, (according to appearances, which have been stated before) then let it stand secure in that situation until you wish to commence dyeing, at which time a copper is to be filled with clear water, then add 2 pounds of potash that has been dissolved in hot water, also one pound of madder and 16 quarts of bran; boil for 15 minutes, then extinguish the fire, allow it to settle a few minutes and empty the clear part into the vat. Then add two pounds of best indigo finely ground. Having filled the vat within 4 inches of the top, rake it well and cover it close. The next morning the vat should be opened and plunged, then cover it close; let it rest one hour, plunge again and let it rest for the same time.

If the dye is in good condition, there will be several quarts of froth on the surface, which will appear of a copper-colored blue, and the liquor of a dark green; in this state the dye is proper to be employed in coloring.

The cloth intended to be dyed should be cleansed from all filth, especially grease, as that would overset the dye even in its best state. Before the cloth is entered into the vat, it must be thoroughly wet in hot water and drained. The quantity of indigo and other ingredients that have been directed, will dye to advantake 60 yards of flannel, which should first be scoured or about one quarter part fulled. Half of that quantity may be dyed at one draught. As soon as the vat is opened for the purpose of dyeing, take off the froth and put it in a convenient vessel; next let down the net, which should be attached to an iron hoop and suspended by three cords. The stick or cross piece is then to be placed about one inch below the surface of the dye, for the purpose of hauling the cloth over it. You will now place the cloth in regular folds, begin at one end and haul it in the dye, keeping it well open till you have drawn through the whole draught; continue hauling the cloth backwards and forwards from end to end for about 20 minutes, during which time it is to be kept entirely under the surface of the dye. After this process, begin at one end and wring it up, then take it on the folding table or boards, and fold it over and over until it becomes blue and even. If this part of the business is neglected, your cloth will be clouded. When the cloth is first taken out of the vat, if the dye is in good order, it will exhibit a green shade, but on being exposed to the air will soon become blue. After each draught of cloth has been dipped twice, take out the cross piece and net, and return the froth back which was taken off, rake and plunge the dye several times, then cover it close. An hour after open the vat, place the net and cross piece, and proceed in dyeing as before until the color is nearly as dark as will at last be required.

The cloth must now be rinsed and pass a second milling. Before you dip the cloth for the last time, you will reheat part of the dye (which is at this time of a bluish brown) in the copper, and when it is ready to boil, all the scum that is formed at the top is taken off with a sieve, then add the same proportions of bran, madder, and potash as before, boil for 15 minutes, the fire is then removed from the copper, and a little cold water put in to stop the boil, allow it to settle for a few minutes, then pour the clear part into the vat, at which time add 2 pounds of finely ground indigo. After this the vat is raked, covered, and some fire put round it: the next day it will be fit to work, which is to be managed as before directed until you have obtained the desired shade. After this, the dye should be suffered to cool, then kept covered close till it is again employed for coloring. The dyer must be careful in hot weather to heat the dye as often as once in six weeks to preserve it. When the dye becomes thick and sizy by much use, the clear part of it must be boiled, the scum taken off, and the clear part returned to the vat; at which time add two quarts of lime water, which will clarify it and cast down the sediment; should the grounds rise, the color will be imperfect, therefore they should be well settled before the goods are admitted.

In dyeing wool in the fleece, it will be necessary to have an additional net, made in a circular form, with meshes about an inch square. The net should have a border fastened to it of stout cotton or linen cloth, with loop holes near the edge, having a cord run through them. When the net is let down into the dye, the border is to be brought over the edge of the vat, and the loop cord secured in many places by hooking it over nails on the outside. After the wool has been scoured clean, rinsed, and nearly dried, it is then thrown loosely in the dye, and stirred about regular with a smooth stick for 20 minutes. The loop cord is then taken from all sides of the vat, and brought together above, forming with the cord a few loops, these are to be put upon a hook attached to a stout strap or rope. The strap is then run over a pulley fixed to the floor, and the net drawn out of the dye; two sticks of timber are then placed across the top of the vat, and a half barrel tub, (bored with holes) rested on them, over the centre of the dye. Next let the net and wool sink into the tub, put on the top of it a circular follower and press it hard with a lever. Then remove the tub, take out the wool, and air it; in this manner proceed to dip and air until it is dark enough.

After coloring deep blue on cloth or wool, the dye may be used for pale blues, which answers a better purpose for that shade when it is weak.

DIRECTION XXV.

For an excellent Black on Woollen.

For 20 yards or 16 pounds of cloth or yarn it will require the following articles,

8 pounds of logwood,
1 pound 4 ounces sumac,
1 pound 4 ounces maple bark,
8 ounces of nutgalls,
3 pounds 8 ounces of copperas,
4 ounces of pearlash,
3 ounces cream of tartar, and
4 ounces of verdigris.

Use the same proportions to dye any number of pounds.

To produce a superior black, you must in the first place dye the cloth a light indigo blue in the warm dye which is to be done before fulling; then full and fit it for coloring.

1. Prepare a kettle with about three barrels of water, then add to it 8 pounds of logwood, one pound four ounces of sumac, the same quantity of maple bark, and 8 ounces of nutgalls powdered fine. It is then brought to boil for one hour and a half; you will then stop it from boiling, and suffer the chips and dye stuff to settle at the bottom; then take out the clear dye liquor, and put it into a clean hogshead, which will be ready for use in one week.

2. In the next place prepare a small kettle with a pail full of warm water, and dissolve in it 3 pounds 8 ounces of copperas, which must be stirred while dissolving, and afterwards the scum is to be taken off.

3. When your logwood liquor has stood for the time above mentioned, or somewhat longer if more convenient; then put about two thirds of it into a clean kettle, bring it to a boil, and put in your cloth and run it while boiling for about one hour. At this time let an-

other person stir up and skim the copperas water, and take about 5 quarts of it and pour into the dye slowly, a little at a time, while you are moving the cloth in the dye; minding not to pour it on the cloth, but rather on the side of the kettle. The cloth is to be run one hour after the copperas liquor is added; then taken out and aired.

4. The dye must now be refreshed with some of the prepared logwood liquor, and also add about one quart of the copperas liquor. It is then brought to a boil, and the cloth put in and run while boiling for one hour, then taken out and aired.

5. You will now add the remainder of the logwood liquor to the dye; also four ounces of pearlash, three ounces of cream of tartar, and four ounces of verdigris, which last must be slacked before hand by putting it in several thicknesses of wet brown paper, and then covering it up in hot embers: it is then to be dissolved in a little of the hot dye liquor, and added to the dye. The dye is now to be brought to a boil, and the cloth put in and run while boiling for one hour; then taken out and aired, and afterwards rinsed and scoured.

DIRECTION XXVI.

To dye a common Black on Woollen.

For 20 yards or 16 pounds of cloth or yarn it will require

2 pounds and a half of copperas,
2 ounces of blue vitriol,
8 pounds of logwood,
2 pounds of fustic.

Use the same proportions to dye any number of pounds.

1. Prepare a kettle with a sufficient quantity of water to admit your woollen to be worked in the dye without

being crowded: bring the water to a scalding heat, then put in the cloth or yarn for a few minutes. When it is wet thoroughly take it out and drain it.

2. In the next place put in two pounds of copperas and 2 ounces of blue vitriol. When both are entirely dissolved, bring the liquor to a gentle boil, stir up the dye and put in the cloth or yarn. (In dyeing of woollen yarn observe that it should often be stirred about in the dye with a stick: the same way also should be practiced in dyeing small quantities of flannel cloth; but it will be found necessary to use a reel to dye cloth in large quantities) run the cloth for one hour, and air it once in that time; it is then to be taken out, aired, and rinsed well.

3. The copperas liquor is now to be emptied away and the kettle rinsed and filled nearly full of water; then add 8 pounds of logwood chips and 2 pounds of fustic chips, which are to boiled about two hours, then add some water and take out the chips.

4. The cloth is now to be put in and run while boiling for half an hour; then take it out and air it. Add half a pound of copperas to the dye, and when it is dissolved, enter the woollen and run it for half an hour longer; then air, rinse, and scour it well.

DIRECTION XXVII.

Another common Black on Woollen.

For 20 yards or 16 pounds of cloth or yarn.

The following receipt may be considered worth attention to those who wish to dye black on woollen in families, as it is attended with but little trouble and expense. The same may be said of the last receipt for dyeing a common black. There are many families who already understand how to dye a good black on woollen;

but there are also many who do not. Some fail in producing a good black, by not using enough dye stuff in proportion for their woollen; others fail by mixing the copperas and logwood together, through the whole course of dyeing the black; and many by not having a sufficient quantity of water at first. There should always be so much dye liquor in dyeing woollen of any color, that the cloth, yarn, or wool, may be moved about loose and free in the dye.

1. Prepare a kettle with a sufficient quantity of water, bring it to a scalding heat, then add 12 ounces of blue vitriol that is pounded; when it is dissolved put in your woollen, and let the liquor boil gently while you are running the cloth, or stirring it about in the dye. When it has been in half an hour, take it up drain and air it, then dip again as before for half an hour. It is then to be taken out and cooled.

2. Now add to the liquor some water and 6 pounds of logwood chips, boil smartly for half an hour, then put in the woollen and run or stir it about for half an hour. It is then to be taken out and cooled.

3. In the next place add either of the following articles to the dye: one pound and a half of madder, or 3 pecks of butternut bark, or a pail full of sumac, or half a bushel of soft maple bark; either one of the kinds will answer. You will then boil and dip until the color pleases. Should you find it not black enough, dissolve a handful of copperas separate in a little of the hot dye liquor, then add it to the dye, and dip the woollen a few minutes longer and it will be completed. Then cool, rinse, and scour it well.

DIRECTION XXVIII.

Green on Woollen.

To dye 1 pound of cloth, yarn, flannel, or any kind of woollen articles, it will require the following ingredients.

1 ounce and a quarter of oil of vitriol,
1 quarter of an ounce of indigo,
1 ounce cream of tartar,
2 ounces of allum,
8 ounces of fustic.

Use the same proportion of articles to dye any number of pounds.

In the first place prepare the chymic or compound of oil of vitriol and indigo, which is made in the following manner.

Take a glazed earthen cup or pot, of a suitable size and put in one ounce aud a quarter of oil of vitriol; then add to it one quarter of an ounce of Spanish flote or best Bengal indigo which is to be pounded fine and sifted; then stir the mixture hastily with a stick, which is necessary in order to mix it well and produce a regular fermentation; this should be done until it has done working: then add half a table spoonful of water, and mix it together and it will be fit for use in one day.

Should the compound not work or ferment after stirring it, you may conclude the oil of vitriol is not good and had better not be used.

Supposing you wish to make more compound than will be wanted for dyeing at one time, you must put it in a glass bottle and stop it close with a wax or glass stopper; in this way it will keep good for a year or more: however those who have had no practice in dyeing green may as well procure only as much oil of vitriol and indigo as will be wanted to dye their woollen at one time; for in this way there will be no chance of making any mistake in using too much or too little. After one trial is made in dyeing green, it will be found afterwards simple and easy. Observe that in the above direction to make the compound, the quantity of oil of vitriol and indigo stated, is calculated to dye one pound of woollen.

Dyeing the Green.

1. Prepare either an iron, brass or copper kettle, with three gallons of water; which is sufficient for one pound of woollen. When the water is scalding hot, add one ounce of cream of tartar, and two ounces of allum; then bring it to boil and put in the woollen, boil it about one hour and a half; stirring it in the liquor occasionally during that time. It is then to be taken out, drained and aired.

2. You will now add some water to the kettle to make up the deficiency caused by boiling; then add to the liquor, two thirds of the compound of oil of vitriol and indigo; mix it well with the liquor, then put in the woollen, keeping the liquor at only a scalding heat, and often moving it about in the dye. When the woollen has been in the dye half an hour, it is to be taken out, aired and rinsed.

3. In the next place add 8 ounces of fustic chips to the liquor, which are to be put loosely in a thin coarse bag, and boiled about an hour and a half. The bag is then to be taken out, and the woollen put in and boiled gently little more than an hour; airing the woollen once in that time. It is then to be taken out and aired.

4. You will find at this time you have produced a green. Should it be found to bear too much on the yellow, then add a little more of the compound to the dye, and put in the woollen again: or if it is too much on the blue shade, boil up a little more fustic in the liquor. In this way you may vary the shade according

to your fancy. If you want a light green, use the less fustic and compound. After it is dyed, air and rinse it.

Another method to dye Green.

1. Prepare the yarn by boiling it in allum and cream of tartar, the same as mentioned in the above receipt for one hour and a half: it is then to be taken out of the liquor and aired.

2. Add to the liquor the same quantity of fustic chips in a bag as mentioned before, and boil it about an hour and a half: then take out the bag and put in the woollen for half an hour: it is then to be taken out and aired.

3. In the next place put in two thirds of the compound: mix it well with the dye liquor, and put in the woollen for half an hour; during which time it should be moved about in the dye at only a scalding heat. It is then to be taken out and aired. Should you find the green not dark enough, add a little more of the compound to the dye and put in the woollen again; then air and rinse.

This last method of dyeing green will answer very well; but is not hardly equal to the one where the blue is put on first: but the last method where the yellow is put on first, is rather more convenient than the other, in particular for new beginners: as in that way they can with more safety produce the desired shade, by putting in but a little of the compound at once; which at the same time tends to produce an even color.

N. B. Green can be dyed as handsome as is commonly done without cream of tartar; but in that case you will use three ounces of allum for every pound of woollen. Observe to mix the compound well in the dye, before the woollen is entered.

DIRECTION XXIX.

Best Bottle Green on Woollen.

After your woollen is dyed green as stated in Direction XXVIII, then take for one pound of woollen, 2 ounces of log-wood chips, which are to be put in loose into a bag and boiled in the dye for a little more than half an hour: then take out the bag, and add half an ounce of copperas. When it is dissolved, put in the woollen and boil it gently for half an hour, stirring it about during the time. It is then to be taken out, cooled and rinsed.

DIRECTION XXX.

Nicaragua-Red on Woollen.

To dye 1 pound of woollen it will require the following articles:

3 ounces of allum,
1 ounce cream of tartar,
8 ounces of Nicaragua.

Use the same proportions to dye any number of pounds.

1. Prepare a brass or copper kettle with about 2 pails of water; bring it to a scalding heat, then add 3 ounces of allum which is pounded, and 1 ounce of fine cream of tartar: bring the liquor to a boil and put in the woollen and let it boil one hour and a half. It is then to be taken out, aired and rinsed and the liquor emptied away.

2. In the next place add to the kettle as much water as before; then add 8 ounces of nicaragua chips, which are to be put loosely into a thin coarse bag and boiled about one hour and a half.

3. Now take out the nicaragua chips and put in the woollen: boil gently for about 1 hour, stirring and air-

ing it during that time. It is then to be taken out cooled and rinsed.

N. B. Should you wish the red to bear on a scarlet color, you will add a little yellow dye liquor to the allum and tartar liquor. The yellow dye may be made from fustic, turmeric, peach leaves, walnut or yellow oak bark.

DIRECTION XXXI.

Madder Red on Woollen.

To dye 1 pound of yarn or flannel it will require the following articles :

3 ounces of allum,
1 ounce cream of tartar,
8 ounces of madder,
½ an ounce of stone lime.

Use the same proportions to dye any number of pounds.

1. Prepare a brass or copper kettle with about five gallons of water; bring the liquor to a scalding heat, then add 3 ounces of allum that is pounded, and one ounce cream of tartar; then bring the liquor to a boil and put in the woollen and boil it for 2 hours. It is then taken out aired and rinsed, and the liquor emptied away.

2. Now prepare the kettle with as much water as before, and add to it 8 ounces of good madder, which should be broken up fine, and well mixed in the water before you put in the woollen. When you have warmed the dye as hot as you can bear the hand in it; then enter the woollen and let it remain in the dye for one hour, during which time the dye must not boil, but only remain at a scalding heat; observing to stir about the woollen constantly while in the dye.

3. When the woollen has been in 1 hour, then bring the dye to a boil for 5 minutes. The woollen is then to be taken out aired and rinsed.

4. Add to the dye half a pint of clear lime water, which is made by slacking about half an ounce of lime to powder; then add water to it and when settled pour the clear part into the dye and mix it well. Now put in your woollen, and stir it about for ten minutes, the dye being only at a scalding heat. It is then to be taken out and rinsed immediately.

N. B. Should you wish the red very bright, add about a quarter of an ounce or nearly $\frac{1}{2}$ a table spoonful of the aqua fortis composition at the time of putting in the madder.

DIRECTION XXXII.

Yellow on Woollen.

To dye one pound of cloth or yarn it will require
3 ounces of allum,
1 ounce cream of tartar, and
1 pound of fustic.

Use the same proportions to dye any number of pounds.

1. Prepare a brass or copper kettle with about four gallons of water; bring it to a scalding heat, then add 3 ounces of pounded allum and 1 ounce of fine cream of tartar; then enter the woollen. Bring it to a boil for one hour and a half. It is then to be taken out cooled and slightly rinsed.

2. In the next place empty away the liquor, and put in as much water as before; then add to it 1 pound of fustic chips cut up fine and put loose in a thin coarse bag; then boil it for two hours.

3. You will then take out the fustic and put in the

woollen, and stir or run it while boiling, for one hour. It is then to be taken out cooled and rinsed.

N. B. Instead of fustic you may use hickory or yellow oak bark, having the dye strong. (See description of those barks.)

DIRECTION XXXIII.

Buff Color on Woollen.

For 16 pounds of cloth.

1. Prepare a brass or copper kettle with a sufficient quantity of water to cover well your woollen; bring the liquor to a scalding heat, then add one pound three quarters of allum and one pound of cream of tartar—bring the liquor to a boil and put in the cloth; run while boiling for one hour and a half: it is then to be taken out and aired.

2. The liquor is then to be emptied away and the kettle filled with as much water as before; then add 3 pounds and a quarter of fustic chips, which is to be put in a bag and boiled about one hour and a half. The bag is then to be taken out and one or two pails full of water added to the dye.

3. Now add 6 ounces of madder to the liquor, which is to be broken up fine and well mixed. Then put in the cloth and run it while boiling for one hour. It is then to be taken out aired and rinsed.

DIRECTION XXXIV.

To dye a Scarlet Red on Woollen Cloth, Yarn, Shawls, Fringe, or any kind of Woollen articles.

Before the directions are given to dye this beautiful colour, it will not be improper to state that a strict attention to neatness, and a careful observance of the rules laid down will be necessary: which, if followed, there will not be the least difficulty to accomplish the dyeing of this color in families.

To dye one pound of woollen, it will require the following articles, which when procured at the druggist's, each kind should be written upon to prevent any mistake in using them.

2 ounces of spirits of nitre,
½ a dram of salt petre (pounded)
2 drams of salamoniac, (pounded)
¼ of an ounce of grained tin.
Also, 1 ounce cream of tartar,
1 ounce of cochineal, (pounded fine)
½ an ounce of starch,
4 drams of turmeric, (pounded.

Use the same proportions to dye any number of pounds.

In the first place prepare the compound of aqua fortis, which should be made at least 2 days before you color the scarlet. It is prepared in the following manner, and the quantity of which is calculated to dye one pound of woollen.

Take a clean glass bottle of a suitable size, put in 2 ounces of spirits of nitre, add to it as much clean rain water, also 2 drams of salamoniac, which is pounded fine, and half a dram of fine salt petre. Shake them together until they are dissolved; then add ¼ of an ounce of grained tin; these small pieces of tin are to be put in one at a time, letting it dissolve before putting in any more, so proceed until the whole is dissolved. After the compound is made then stop the bottle close with a wax or glass stopper. In using it be careful to take the clear liquor only.

Directions to grain the Tin.

Melt block tin over a fire, then pour it from a distance above of four or five feet slowly into a bason of cold water. By this process the tin will be cast into thin and loose parts, and is then fit to be dissolved as beforementioned. Tin is oftentimes procured at the druggists already grained or granulated; in that case it is ready to be dissolved in the spirits of nitre or aqua fortis.

Dyeing the Scarlet.

1. Prepare a tin, brass, or copper kettle with about five gallons of clean soft water; bring it nearly to a scalding heat, then add one ounce of cream of tartar, one third of an ounce of cochineal which is finely pounded and sifted through gauze, and four drams of pounded turmeric. Make a quick fire, and when the liquor almost boils add nearly half of the clear compound already prepared, and mix it well with the dye.

2. The liquor is now brought to a boil. The cloth, yarn, or woollen articles being before well cleansed, wet and drained, is now to be entered: dip it while boiling for one hour and a half. If it is yarn or garments, they are to be continually moved or stirred with a stick, and if cloth where it is a sufficient quantity, it is to be run briskly on the reel.

3. The woollen is now to be taken out, drained cooled, and rinsed in cold water. Empty out the dye, and add as much clean soft water as before; then dissolve half an ounce of starch in a little warm water, and add to the water in the kettle.

4. Bring the water to a scalding heat and skim it; then add two thirds of an ounce of cochineal being the remainder, also add a little before it boils the remainder of the prepared tin composition, which you must be careful to use only the clear part, and when put in the dye it is to be well mixed.

5. The dye is now brought to a boil, and the woollen entered, which is to be stirred about as before. Boil

it about one hour and a half: it is then to be taken out and aired, then rinsed and dried.

N. B. Fulled cloth must be napped and sheared before it is dyed scarlet. After it is dyed and rinsed, then tenter it, and lay the nap with a clean brush. Press it in clean papers, not very hot as that would tarnish the color.

DIRECTION XXXV.

Scarlet Red.

To dye 20 yards or 16 pounds of Yarn or cloth, it will require the following articles.

2 pounds of spirits of nitre,
2 ounces salamoniac, (finely pounded)
1 ounce sal. nitre,
4 ounces of grained tin.

The above ingredients form the composition of aqua fortis; and is mixed as follows. Take a glass bottle of a suitable size, and put in the spirits of nitre: then add to it, 2 pounds of pure soft water and mix it together: then also add 2 ounces of salamoniac finely pounded, and one ounce of sal. nitre and shake them together until the salts are dissolved. In the next place 4 ounces of grained tin is to be added gradually; dropping in one by one and waiting for one to dissolve before putting in the second. When it is thus gradually dissolved, the composition is completed, and the day after it is made, it will be ready for use. When the composition is kept on hand, it must be kept stopped close with a wax or glass stopper.

The following articles will be wanted to dye the above quantity of woollen.

14 ounces of cochineal, (finely pounded and sifted)
12 ounces of cream of tartar,
4 ounces of turmeric, (pounded.)

Dyeing the Scarlet.

1. After the cloth is fitted for the press, having it well cleansed and wet with hot water, and the tin, brass or copper kettle perfectly cleaned, then fill it with pure soft water, and add a peck of wheat bran, which is to be enclosed in a bag and tied closely. Let the water boil a few minutes; then take out the bag and add 12 ounces of cream of tartar that is pounded fine: let it boil a few minutes, then add one third of the cochineal, and 4 ounces of turmeric, which is to be put in a bag.

2. Make a quick fire, then add nearly half of the clear composition, already prepared, and mix it well with the dye which at this time will change to a blood red. The liquor is now brought to a boil, then dip the cloth, while boiling, for one hour and a half; keeping it well spread and running it briskly on the reel.

3. The cloth is now to be taken up, drained and cooled; then rinsed in cold water. Next, empty out the dye. Add fresh and clear soft water as before; bring it to a scalding heat, then add the remainder of the cochineal: also add, a little before it boils, the remainder of the clear composition, and when put in the dye it is to be well mixed.

4. Bring the dye to a boil and enter the woollen and run it one hour and a half, while boiling. It is then to be taken out and aired, then rinsed and the nap laid with a clean brush while wet, on the bars.

N. B. Particular care must be observed in dyeing scarlet or other bright fancy colors, (including all light shades) that the kettles, reel, sticks, and every implement employed, should be made perfectly clean and free from any darkening substance.

DIRECTION XXXVI.

To Dye a Crimson Color on Woollen Cloth, Yarn, Flannel, Shawls, Network, Fringe, &c.

For one pound of woollen it will require the following articles, viz :

1 ounce cream of tartar,
2 ounces of allum,
1 ounce of cochineal,
2 drams salmoniac,
$\frac{1}{4}$ of an ounce of pearlash,
6 ounces of wheat bran.

Use the same proportions to dye any number of pounds.

1. Prepare a brass or copper kettle with about 4 gallons of rain water, or soft spring water; bring it to scalding heat, then add one ounce of fine cream of tartar, and 2 ounces of allum, pounded fine. The liquor is now brought to a boil, and the woollen entered and stirred about in the dye, while boiling, for one hour and a half.

2. In the next place take out the woollen and air it; then rinse it slightly in clean water. Empty away the liquor and add as much clean soft water as before.—When the water has become blood warm, add about 6 ounces of wheat bran, tied up in a bag.

3. Now bring the liquor to a moderate heat, and take off the scum as it rises to the top: then take out the bag and add 1 ounce of cochineal that is pounded fine and sifted. The dye is now brought to a boil, and the woollen put in and stirred or turned round while boiling for one hour; then take it out and rinse it in clear cold water.

4. The dye is now to be emptied away and as much water added as before. When the liquor is as warm as the hand can be endured in it, dissolve therein 2 drams of salmoniac which is pounded fine; then enter the

woollen and move it about hastily for 5 minutes; it is then to be taken out and drained.

5. Now add one quarter of an ounce of pearlash, or about 2 tea spoonfulls: mix it well with the liquor, and when the dye is almost scalding hot put in the woollen and move it round for about 10 minutes: it is then to be taken out, aired and rinsed; which completes a crimson that is permanent and beautiful.

DIRECTION XXXVII.

Orange Color on Woollen.

To dye 1 pound of cloth, yarn, or garments, it will require

1 ounce of anatto or otter, and
2 ounces of pearlash.

1. Prepare a brass or copper kettle with about 2½ gallons of water, then add to it 1 ounce of anatto, which should be cut up fine and put loosely into a bag as thin as a strainer: also add to the water 2 ounces of pearlash; then boil it for about 1 hour.

2. Instead of putting the anatto into a bag, you may put the fine pieces loose in the kettle and boil it for the same length of time; then let it settle a few hours and pour off the clear part into another kettle: throw away the settlings and put the clear liquor back as before.

3. Before you dip the woollen in the dye, it should be wet with hot water and drained: then bring the dye to a scalding heat and put in the woollen, which is to be moved about in the dye 1 hour at nearly a boiling heat. It is then to be taken out, aired and rinsed.

DIRECTION XXXVIII.

Cinnamon Color on Woollen.

For 24 yards of thin cloth.

1. Prepare a kettle with a sufficient quantity of water, then add 3 pounds of ground camwood and 3 pecks of butternut bark; let it boil a few minutes, then enter

the cloth and run it, while boiling, for one hour. It is then to be taken out and aired.

2. Now put in the cloth again and run it for the same length of time as before. Should it not be as dark as you wish, take out the bark and dissolve a little copperas in some hot water, and add it to the dye; then run the cloth a few minutes and it is finished. Then cool and rinse it.

DIRECTION XXXIX.

To Dye a Dark Cinnamon, London Brown and British Mud.

For 20 yards fulled cloth, or 26 yards thin cloth.

1. Prepare a kettle with a sufficient quantity of water, bring it to a moderate heat, and wet the cloth thoroughly; then take it up and let it drain: add 6 pounds of camwood and half a pound of fustic chips. Let it boil half an hour, then dip your cloth while boiling, for one hour and a half. It is then to be taken out and aired.

2. Now add some cold water to the dye, and about half a gill of oil of vitriol, which is to be mixed with a little cold water before it is added; also add a small handfull of blue vitriol and as much copperas. When these are entirely dissolved and well mixed with the liquor, bring the dye to a boil and run the cloth about 1 hour; the dark cinnamon is then obtained. It is then to be taken out, aired and rinsed.

3. To produce a London Brown, you will proceed by emptying away the liquor and adding as much water as before; then add 3 pounds of logwood chips (put in a bag) which is to be boiled one hour, then take out the bag and add 12 ounces of copperas; bring the dye to a boil and run the cloth about 20 minutes. By ad-

ding some more logwood liquor and copperas, you will obtain a British Mud. Then take up, cool and rinse.

DIRECTION XL.

Olive Brown on Woollen.

For 20 yards or 16 pounds of cloth.

1. Prepare a kettle with a sufficient quantity of water; when it has become warm add 12 ounces of cream of tartar and 1 pound 12 ounces of allum; then bring the water to a boil and run the cloth while boiling, for one hour and a half. It is then to be taken out, aired and rinsed.

2. In the next place empty out the liquor and fill the kettle with water as before. Then add 6 pounds of fustic chips and $1\frac{1}{2}$ pounds of logwood chips, which are to be enclosed in a thin coarse bag and boiled about 1 hour and a half; then take out the bag and refresh the dye with some water and add one pound of madder, which is to be broken up fine and well mixed in the dye.

3. The cloth is now to be entered and run at a scalding heat for 1 hour; then let the dye boil, and run it 15 minutes longer. It is then to be taken out, aired and rinsed.

4. Again refresh the dye with some water, then add 3 ounces of the compound of oil of vitriol and indigo, which is to be well mixed with the dye. Bring the dye to a boil and dip the cloth for 20 minutes. It is then to be taken up, aired and rinsed.

5. The dye is now to be refreshed with water, then add one pound of logwood chips (put in a bag) which is to be boiled half an hour; then take out the chips and add 8 ounces of copperas; run and boil the cloth 15 minutes, then take up, cool and rinse.

DIRECTION XLI.

Olive Brown on Woollen.

For 20 yards or 16 pounds of cloth.

1. Prepare a kettle with a sufficient quantity of water, then add 6 pounds of fustic chips and boil it well for 1 hour. The cloth is then to be entered and run at a boiling heat, for 1 hour. It is then to be taken out and aired.

2. The dye is now to be refreshed with water, then add 1 bushel of butternut bark; boil it moderately one hour, then enter your cloth and run it for about 1 hour. It is then to be taken out and aired. Take the chips and bark out of the dye and add 4 ounces of copperas; when it is dissolved, enter your cloth and run till it suits your mind; then cool and rinse it.

DIRECTION XLII.

Olive on Woollen.

For 16 pounds of cloth.

1. Prepare a kettle with about 2 barrels of water, bring it to a scalding heat, then add 1 pound 12 ounces of allum, and 6 ounces cream of tartar. When it is dissolved bring it to a boiling heat, then enter the cloth and run it while boiling, for one hour and a half. It is then to be taken out and aired.

2. In the next place refresh the dye with some water, then add 5 pounds of fustic chips, 6 ounces of pounded turmeric and three ounces of madder; all of which are to be put loosely in a coarse bag and boiled for about one hour and a half. Take out the bag and enter the cloth and run it for one hour. It is then to be taken out and aired.

3. The dye is now to be refreshed with water, then

add 2 pounds and a half of logwood chips, (put in a bag) which is to be boiled about half an hour, then take out the bag and add 6 ounces of pearlash: enter the cloth and run it while boiling for 1 hour. It is then to be taken out, aired and rinsed.

Should the color not be dark enough after airing it, add some copperas and run again till it pleases.

DIRECTION XLIII.

Navy Blue on Woollen.

For 20 yards or 16 pounds of cloth.

1. Prepare a kettle with 2 barrels of water, bring it to a scalding heat, then add 12 ounces of copperas, 3 ounces of allum, $1\frac{1}{2}$ ounces of verdigris $1\frac{1}{2}$ ounces cream of tartar; then bring the water to a boil and enter the cloth: run it while boiling, for 1 hour. It is then to be taken out, aired and rinsed.

2. In the next place empty away the liquor and fill up with water as before; then add $4\frac{1}{2}$ pounds of logwood chips, (put in a bag) boil it for $1\frac{1}{2}$ hours; the bag is then to be taken out and the dye refreshed with water. Now add 6 ounces of madder, which is to be broken up fine and well mixed in the dye; it is then to be brought to a boil and the cloth put in and run while boiling, for about half an hour—then taken out and aired.

3. Now add to the dye 6 ounces of blue vitriol and 3 ounces of pearlash; mix it well with the liquor, then run the cloth while boiling, for about 20 minutes. It is then to be taken out, aired and rinsed.

DIRECTION XLIV.

Navy Blue on Woollen.

For 20 yards or 16 pounds of yarn or cloth.

1. Prepare a kettle with a sufficient quantity of water, bring it to a scalding heat, then wet the cloth or yarn and let it drain. Add to the water one pound of copperas, 2 ounces of blue vitriol and 1 ounce of allum. When it is dissolved bring the liquor to a boil, and run the woollen for 1 hour. It is then to be taken out, aired and rinsed.

2. In the next place empty away the liquor and fill up again with water; then add 5 pounds of logwood chips. Boil it for 1 hour, then run the woollen for 15 minutes, then take up and air it. Now add a little blue vitriol, then dip the woollen. In this way add and dip until you get the shade to your mind.

DIRECTION XLV.

Purple on Woollen.

For 20 yards or 16 pounds of yarn or cloth.

1. Prepare a kettle with a sufficient quantity of water to cover the cloth or yarn, then add 3 pounds of camwood and the liquor of 9 pounds of logwood.

2. Bring the dye to a boiling heat, then enter the woollen, (which must be wet in hot water before hand and drained) run it for about half an hour while boiling. It is then to be taken out and aired.

3. In the next place add to the dye four ounces of blue vitriol that is pounded; when it is dissolved then run the cloth for half an hour. It is then to be taken up and aired. Now add some copperas liquor to the dye, mix it well, then run again till the color suits; it is then to be aired and rinsed.

DIRECTION XLVI.

Snuff color on Woollen.

For 20 yards or 16 pounds of yarn or cloth.

1. Prepare a kettle with a sufficient quantity of water, when it has become warm, wet your cloth and drain it, then add one pound of copperas, bring the liquor to a scalding heat and take off the scum that rises on the top. When the liquor begins to boil, enter and run the cloth one hour, (airing it once in that time.) It is then to be taken up, aired, and rinsed.

2. The liquor is now to be emptied out, and the kettle filled again with fresh water; then add 8 pounds of fustic chips, half a bushel of butternut bark, 1 pound of camwood, and half a pound of madder.

3. The dye is then to be boiled moderately 2 hours, and the cloth run for half an hour; it is then taken out and aired. Dissolve half a pound of copperas in a little of the hot liquor, then add it to the dye, and run your cloth until the color suits.

DIRECTION XLVII.

Snuff Brown and London Smoke.

For 20 yards fulled cloth or 26 yards thin cloth.

1. Prepare a kettle with a sufficient quantity of water when it has become nearly scalding hot, wet the cloth and drain it. Then add to the liquor two pounds of copperas, bring it to a scalding heat and skim the dye. When the copperas is dissolved, enter the cloth and run it while moderately boiling, for one hour; it is then to be taken out aired and rinsed.

2. In the next place empty out the liquor, and fill the kettle again with fresh water; then add ten pounds of fustic chips, and one bushel of butternut bark; boil moderately for three hours, then enter the cloth, and

run and air it several times for one hour, or until the strength is well out of the dye; it is then to be taken up and aired. To darken the color first take out the bark and chips, then add half a pound of copperas: when it is dissolved run the cloth for 15 minutes, and it will be finished.

3. To produce a London smoke, add the liquor of four pounds of logwood before the copperas is added, then bring it to a boil and run for one hour, then cool and rinse.

DIRECTION XLVIII.

Light Drab on Woollen.

For 20 yards or 16 pounds of cloth.

1. Prepare a kettle with a sufficient quantity of water, then add a bushel of white ash bark, and one quarter of a pound of fustic chips; boil it for one hour, then take out the bark and fustic.

2. Now add as much water as evaporated in boiling, then dissolve a handful of copperas in some of the hot liquor by itself, and add a part of it to the dye, mix it well and bring it to a boil, then run your cloth for about half an hour. It is now to be taken out quick and aired.

3. If you wish the color darker, add a little more of the copperas liquor to the dye, and mix it well, then run the cloth until the shade is to your mind. It is then to be taken out, aired, and rinsed.

DIRECTION XLIX.

To dye a Drab color on Woollen, (with nutgalls.)

1. Prepare a kettle with a sufficient quantity of wa-

ter, bring it to a scalding heat and wet your cloth, then take it up and let it drain.

2. In the next place add five table spoonfulls of finely pounded nutgalls, and boil for half an hour; then enter the cloth and run while boiling, for half an hour; it is then to be taken out and aired.

3. Now add to the dye half a table spoonfull of allum; let it boil a few minutes, then skim off the filth that rises at the top. Run your cloth again for half an hour, then take out and air. Add a tea spoonfull of copperas, then run again until the color suits your mind, then air and rinse.

DIRECTION L.

Silver Gray on Woollen.

To dye one pound of cloth or yarn it will require the following articles.

Half an ounce of copperas,
Half an ounce cream of tartar.
3 ounces of logwood,
2 ounces of sumac.

Use the same proportions to dye any number of pounds.

1. Prepare a kettle with about 4 gallons of water, then take two ounces of the shoots and leaves of sumac that are cured and cut up fine, and three ounces of logwood chips; put them loosely into a thin coarse bag and boil it for about one hour, then take the bag out.

2. Now add to the dye half an ounce cream of tartar, then bring it to a boil, and put in the woollen for one hour: it is then to be taken out and aired.

3. In the next place refresh the dye with water, then add to it half an ounce of copperas; when it is dissolved bring the dye to a moderate boil, then enter the wool-

len and move it round for twenty minutes; it is then to be taken out, aired, and rinsed.

DIRECTION LI.

Indigo Blue on Wool or Linen, (as practiced in many families.)

1. To color 6 pounds of wool, or 5 pounds of linen yarn, put two pailsfull of chamberlye into a clean tub, then dissolve 4 ounces of potash, (or instead of it 6 ounces of pearlash) in one quart of hot water; put this in the tub, mix it and let it stand for six days. Then pour off the clear part into a kettle, until you come to the settlings. The settlings will now be thrown away, and the tub rinsed; you will then pour the clear liquor back into the tub again.

2. Take 4 ounces of indigo, and two ounces of madder, put them into a thin bag, and put it in the tub, rubbing it well 4 or 5 times in the course of the day. You will now put the yarn or wool under the dye for 6 hours, then take it out, wring and air it. If it is not dark enough put it in again and proceed as before, until it is to your mind.

N. B. When the dye grows weak, add more dye stuff and let the proportion be the same as at first directed, although the quantity used will not be as much. Spanish Flote, or best Bengal Indigo, is to be preferred for this dye.

DESCRIPTION

OF

DYE-WOODS AND DRUGS.

NUTGALLS.—Of the gall nut there are different kinds; some inclining to white, some ash-colored, and others to a blueish cast. They also differ in size and are either round or irregular, heavy or light, smooth or knotted. Those which are small, knotted and heavy and of a dark color are esteemed the best; they are of a very astringent nature, and of great use in dyeing black, grays, &c. on wool, silk and cotton. Galls are used to great advantage as a basis in the preparation of many colors, as the astringent quality which they possess becomes affixed to the body of the stuffs; and when dipped in the dye, the coloring matter immediately adheres to it.

Sumac will supply the place of galls, in dyeing various colors, if used in a sufficient quantity to produce a liquor of an equal strength.

MADDER.—This is an important and valuable plant; which is used in dyeing red, cinnamon, &c. The common, or crop madder is cultivated among the Dutch in Zealand, where it is prepared and ground for exportation. The plant has rough narrow leaves, set round the joints of the stem in the form of a star.— The root which is the only part made use of, is long and slender, of a red color, both on the outside and within, excepting a whitish pith that runs through the middle of it. The only precaution in selecting the common ground madder, is that it should appear of a bright yellowish red-brown, and should smell sweet and fresh.

The madder plant may be cultivated in many parts of the United States to advantage. It is three years after the first root is set in the ground, before it comes to maturity: they may be placed 4 feet apart in the first setting them in the ground, and should be hoed the first year to keep them clear from weeds. If they are planted on a rich deep soil, which is much the best, the roots will extend to the depth of two feet or more, and yield more abundantly than almost any other vegetable. The time of taking them out of the ground is in the months of September and October, they are then carefully assorted and washed in clean cold water and dryed by a stove heat, ready for pounding. The first pounding separates and brings into the form of a powder the smallest fibres of the roots, with the skin or husk of the larger ones, and any earth which may have been left adhering thereto. This powder being sifted, is then packed separately in casks and sold at a low price and used for cheap dark colors.

A second pounding separates about one third of the remaining part of the larger roots, and this being sifted and packed separately, is called ordinary powder. The third and last pounding comprehends the residue and bright part of the roots; this is called crop madder, which produces the best of reds. This kind of madder is as yet rather scarce in this country.

Madder gives to woollen cloth, prepared with allum and tartar, the most durable of all reds, though not so bright as the cochineal scarlet; yet the red of madder has this important advantage, by enduring to be washed with soap, without producing any material change of color: whereas the cochineal scarlet by the same means used, becomes tarnished.

Those who dye the best madder red, are very careful to keep the liquor of a heat considerably below that of boiling, encreasing the fire towards the end, so that it may boil only a minute or two just before the woollen is taken out. Should the liquor be suffered to boil for a long time, it would extract the light brown matter contained in madder, which would change it to a dull dark red.

NICARAGUA.—This wood is considerably used for dyeing cheap reds, & other colors throughout this country? it is almost as red and heavy as the true Brazil-wood, but will not generally afford half as much color. Nicaragua differs much in quality, for some of it will dye twice as much as others. The best kind grows near Santa Martha, in South-America; that which is the soundest and appears of a yellowish red, on cutting it, is generally allowed to be of a good quality.

BRAZIL, OR RED WOOD.—This kind of dye-wood is imported from different parts of South-America and Japan; it varies much in quality from having been more or less exposed to air. A small quantity of this wood is sometimes used to advantage in finishing madder reds, or in place of cochineal in dyeing cheap scarlets,

CAMWOOD.—This wood affords a coloring matter that is permanent, when the dye is imparted to woollen and withstands the effects of air and common acids, much better than most other dye-woods.

The appearance of this wood on first splitting it, is of a bright redish orange, and has a pungent smell, but after it has been exposed to the air the color changes to a dull red. In preparing it for boiling, it should be chipped fine or ground, but the last method is far the best. In selecting that which is ground choose that of a yellowish red complexion. That which is of a dark red will afford no good color.

LOGWOOD.—This kind of dye wood is well known from its being so generally used in dying throughout this country. It is valuable in many respects, particularly for dyeing black; it is also useful in altering the shades of various colors. The dye itself, produced from this wood soon fades, but on being united with other materials it affords many shades of color, not easily obtained with other woods or drugs. For this reason, together with its low price, the use of it is rendered desirable, especially from its being capable of giving to cloths a soft and velvet hue. This and other dye woods when chipped and used for dyeing, should be enclosed in a thin coarse bag to prevent the chips sticking to the cloth; as that in many cases would not only injure the quality of the cloth, but cloud or spot it, especially if the strength of the chips was not all out before the cloth was entered in the dye. This wood comes over in large logs, cleared from the bark. The best of it is very hard, compact, heavy and of a red color.

FUSTIC.—This kind of dye wood is a species of mulberry, which grows in the West Indies and South-America, and comes in logs; it is of a deep sulphur color, which it readily gives out, both to spirits and water. This wood is extensively used in dyeing yellow, drab, olive and green, also in many other colors. The color of fustic is rendered more permanent by using sumac with it. The best kind is solid, heavy and free from sap and powder post.

WELD.—This plant is raised in great quantities in England and France, and might be cultivated to advantage in many parts of the United States. It is much used by the calico-printers in Europe, for their most durable and fine yellows on chintz. As yet there has no plant, or any kind of drug been found except Quercitron, that will compare with it in affording bright and permanent yellows. The preparation for dyeing yellow on wool with weld is allum and cream of tartar; on cotton allum and a small proportion of blue vitriol.

T URMERIC.—This is the root of the curcuma, and affords a rich color, and surpasses every other yellow coloring matter in point of beauty; but has little attraction either to mordants or stuffs: of course the color has no solidity and soon fades. It is sometimes used to give an orange tint to scarlet, where a flame color is wanted, and is also employed in dyeing some colors on silk.

PASTEL, OR WOAD.—This plant is distinguished by two

kinds, the seeds of one is violet, the other yellow, the former is preferred. The woad begins to ripen in June, and is known to be ripe by its falling down and growing yellow, it is then gathered, and the ground cleared from weeds, which is carefully repeated each crop. The plant, after being cut down, is washed in a stream, and then dried as speedily as possible; it is next carried to the mill to be ground and reduced to a paste. It is then formed into heaps and after pressing the paste well with the hands and feet, it is beat down and made smooth with a shovel. An outward crust soon forms which becomes dark colored: when it cracks, great care must be taken to close it again. At the end of a fortnight these heaps are opened, beaten and well mixed. It is then made into round balls and dried in the sun.

Woad affords without the assistance of indigo, a blue of considerable permanency, but is destitute of brightness. The use of Woad as a dye, is at present nearly abandoned, and is now chiefly employed for the purpose of fermenting the blue dye for woollen. Of late some dyers are inclined to believe that other cheap vegetables the growth of our country might supply the place of Woad in that respect.

ROCOU & ANNATTO.—Rocou is a kind of dry paste brought from South America. It gives an orange color to stuffs in general, but is not permanent.

Annatto is an ingredient of the same kind, only more pure and fine, and does not require more than half of the quantity as that of rocou in dyeing. It is principally employed for dyeing silk and sometimes for cotton.

INDIGO.—This is the most extraordinary and useful of all dyeing drugs; from its affording a blue color, that withstands in a very great degree the action of acids and alkalies. For these reasons indigo blue is chosen and very properly for dying various descriptions of goods that require to be often washed. Indigo is cultivated and manufactured in South America, the East-Indies, Isle of France, Louisiana, Carolinas, &c. The best is brought from Bengal; and comes in pieces about two inches square.

That which is stamped with letters is generally the best. The first quality of Guatimala Indigo is next to be preferred, and will produce as fine a color as that of Bengal, but affords not so great a quantity of coloring matter.

The indigo brought from the isle of France, St. Domingo, New-Orleans and Carolina, are of a harder kind, and contain a greater proportion of gross and impure materials than the kinds before mentioned; however they will answer to dye middling, and low-priced blues on cotton and woollen, but are the best adapted for linen.

METHOD OF PROVING INDIGO.—Take a small piece of any kind of indigo; place it on a red-hot iron or coal of fire; if the indigo is good, it will melt or rather fry out like wax, and a beautiful crimson smoke will arise from it; the piece will also be nearly consumed, and a white substance remain like ashes.—If it is of a poor quality it will fry out but little, and a hard substance will remain, and sometimes nearly as large as the piece before tried.

Good indigo is known by its floating on water, the more it sinks the more it may be suspected of being adultered; its color should be of a deep blue, bordering on the violet, and on rubbing it with the finger nail, should appear of a copper color.—For dyeing green on woollen, the best Spanish Flote indigo is to be preferred.

COCHINEAL.—This insect affords an important and valuable coloring matter, for dyeing crimson and scarlet. The fluids of this insect are colored red, by feeding upon the red juices of the prickly pear of South America. Cochineal will retain its properties a great number of years, if it is kept dry, in a glass bottle stopped tight. That which is good, and has been well prepared, is plump and of a greyish color inclining to purple: that which has been damaged by sea water, appears of a dull crimson hue and is useless.

TIN.—This kind of metal is produced from the mines of Cornwall in England, which when refined is called block-tin. It is used in dyeing scarlet, crimson, yellow &c. by first dissolving it in spirits of nitre or aqua-fortis. It has been found necessary to grain the tin before it can be dissolved, which is done by melting and poring it from a distance into cold water, which separates it into small pieces. Tin is often imported in a grained state.

AQUA-FORTIS.—This is a corrosive liquor made by distilling purified nitre with calcined vitriol, or rectified oil of vitriol in a strong heat.

OIL OF VITRIOL.—This is a strong sulphuric acid, and among other uses in dyeing, it is employed to dissolve indigo for saxon-blue, green &c. on silk and woollen, and sometimes for cotton. It should be as clear as water, of a bright color, and weigh about 29 ounces to the wine pint.

SALAMONIAC.—This is a volatile salt made with soot, a little sea-salt, and the urine of cattle. Some chymists imitate it by adding one part of common salt to five of urine, with which some again mix that quantity of soot. Should it accidentally contain any iron, it will darken a scarlet. It can be proved in that respect with the tincture of galls.

SPIRITS OF SALT.—The chemical term of this is muriatic acid, which is the acid of sea salt.

ALLUM.—Nature affords no perfect allum, but affords the materials for it, in many kinds of ores and mineral substances. It is a fossil salt or white mineral, separated from the earth by washing it with water, which being impregnated with its salts, is afterwards boiled and evaporated. Allum is a valuable mordant or preparation for many colors, and for almost all kinds of stuffs, whether of a vegetable or of an animal production.

COPPERAS OR GREEN VITRIOL.—Copperas is a vitrolic substance extracted from iron. It is used as a mordant or preparation for black and other dark colors ; also for darkening various shades, wherein is used astringent vegetables, such as sumac, alder bark, nutgalls, &c. Copperas should be free from rust, and kept in neither a very wet or dry exposed situation.

BLUE VITRIOL.—This ingredient is made from a combination of oil of vitriol and copper. It is used to advantage as a mordant or preparation for dyeing black and other colors ; also in fixing colors and saddening them.

VERDIGRIS.—This drug is the rust of copper, produced by rubbing grapes or other vegetable acids on copper, which causes it to dissolve slowly.

This preparation is made in large quantities in Europe, particularly in some parts of France. It should be chosen of a bright green color throughout, with no white or black specks or stalks of the grape. It is used to advantage in dyeing some colors, especially black.

ARGOL, OR CREAM OF TARTAR.—This drug is formed by nature into a hard and almost stony separation, from a vegetable juice after fermentation. The common tartar is the produce of wine, being found in large masses adhering to the bottom and sides of casks, in which that liquor has long been kept.—This material is useful in fixing many colors on woollen, and when used with allum, prevents the latter from congealing or forming into chrystals.

POT & PEARLASH.—Potash is a caustic vegetable alkali, which is made by burning vegetables to ashes. They are first leached with water, then evaporated by boiling until the salts are produced.

Pearlash is of much the same nature as potash differing only by a process of baking it in an oven.

Of Barks and Plants useful in Dyeing.

ALDER BARK.—This bark is not much used in dyeing in America, except in the small domestic dye. It possesses a coloring matter, and when applied to cotton or wool, previously prepared, in a solution of allum will produce a lasting brownish yellow. With a preparation of copperas and allum, and afterwards dipped in a strong liquor extracted from the bark, it will produce a brown, and by being prepared with copperas only, will assist to produce a black. Alder bark may be considered nearly as valuable in assisting to form a black as sumac.

ARSMART.—This weed grows in plenty in many parts of the United States, and is generally found at the sides of roads and fences. This plant affords a yellow dye that is durable, when applied to woollen, and more permanent than fustic when imparted to cotton. It is found necessary in preparing it for dyeing yellow, to use as much of it as can be crowded under the water, and allow it to soak in a warm place for three or four days; afterwards it must be brought to a scalding heat. Woollen is first prepared by boiling it one hour in allum water, using 4 ounces of allum to a pound of woollen, then dipped in the yellow dye. Cotton or linen are to be first soaked in the same proportion of allum and water (only warm) over night, then wrung and dipped in the yellow dye, at little less than a scalding heat.

BUTTERNUT BARK.—This bark is esteemed from its affording a durable color, and a great variety of shades. The coloring matter is extracted to the best advantage, by soaking the bark in water a few hours before you begin to color: during which time the water should not be suffered to get hot. Enter the woollen when the liquor is warm, (having the bark in the kettle) keep a gentle fire under it, and bring it slowly to a scalding heat, airing it once in half an hour. You will proceed to dip and air in this manner, until the strength of the bark is exhausted; observing not to suffer the liquor to boil, as that would injure the color. By using a great proportion of bark, and adding copperas to the liquor, after the strength of the bark is extracted, and the bark taken out of the dye, you may obtain a very handsome dark brown, equal to a British mud. The bark is best when used green. To dye cotton with this bark, the cotton is first prepared in allum, using 4 ounces to the pound, and only as much water as will cover the cotton, being as warm as you can bear the hand in it. Let it soak over night, then wring it out and dip in the bark dye until it suits your mind.

BIRCH BARK.—The bark of the black birch, dyes a nankeen color on cotton and linen with an allum preparation. After boiling the bark it should be strained, and suffered to cool so that you can bear the hand in it, then dip the cotton till the color suits.

HEMLOCK BARK.—This bark affords a coloring matter, which with an allum preparation produces a durable light reddish brown on wool, when the dye is made strong, and a nankeen color on cotton, but not very permanent on the latter. When the wool or cotton is prepared with copperas, it produces dark drab and slate colors.

MAPLE BARK.—The bark of the soft maple produces a durable cinnamon color on wool, and also on cotton, by first boiling the woollen in allum water for one hour, then boil up a separate and strong dye of the bark and dip it. Cotton is to be first soaked in warm allum water several hours, then handled in the bark dye, at a little less than a scalding heat. When the woollen or cotton is prepared in copperas liquor, it produces slate colors, light or dark, according to the strength of the preparation and dye liquor.

WALNUT, OR HICKORY BARK.—This bark produces a bright yellow and far more durable than that of fustic, either when applied to cotton or wool. Woollen is prepared for dyeing by boiling it one hour in allum water, using 4 ounces of allum to a pound of wool. In the next place, make a strong dye of the bark and dip the woollen until it is to your mind.

Cotton is dyed by handling it in allum water of the same strength, but only warm: then let it soak in it over night. It is then to be wrung and dipped in the dye until it suits. The dye for woollen is to be nearly boiling hot, but for cotton only as warm as the hand can be borne in at the time of dipping it.

N. B. By dyeing cotton or linen, a light indigo blue first, then alluming it, and afterwards dipping it in the walnut bark dye with a little blue vitriol, you will obtain a green.

YELLOW OAK BARK.—This species of bark affords a more durable yellow on cotton, linen or woollen than any other native plant, bark or root that has yet been discovered in the U. States. The bark appears to consist of three coats, viz: The outside coat which age hardens and becomes almost black—the middle coat, in which the coloring matter mostly resides, is of a yellow color. The inside part is rather hard and fibrous, and therefore does not contain much coloring matter.

The outside coat of this bark, affords a coloring matter but is of a yellowish brown, therefore it must be separated and taken off by shaving, and thrown away. The remainder must be dried and ground, which will form it partly into powder, and the rest into stringy fibres. The bark thus prepared, will yield far more coloring matter than either fustic or weld. In trade and commerce, this bark is called Quercitron, and is now sold in New-York for exportation, from 45 to 60 dollars per ton. To produce a good color with the bark, it should not be boiled, but first steeped in cold water, afterwards the strength is to be extracted at a scalding heat. The method of dyeing cotton and woollen with this bark, in other respects is the same as has been stated for dyeing yellow with hickory bark.

SUMAC.—The common sumac is a natural production of the United States, the stalks of which afford a yellow dye, with an allum preparation. The shoots and leaves have another kind of coloring matter much like that of nutgalls, which renders it valuable in dyeing cotton and woollen drab and slate colors. Of late it is much used in dyeing black and many other colors. Sumac should be cut in the last part of summer, or in the month of September, taking that of only one season's growth: it should then be dried like hay and packed away. Before it is used, it should be cut up fine or ground, using the shoots and leaves mixed together. After boiling sumac for dyeing, the liquor should be strained before the stuffs are dipped.

PEACH LEAVES.—It is found that the leaves of the peach tree afford a yellow color more durable than that of fustic. These leaves are not much used, except in the small domestic dye. The leaves are gathered and used while green. The color is extracted and the stuffs dyed in the same manner as directed in the description of arsmart.

LOMBARDY POPLAR.—The bark and shoots of this tree produce a tolerable good yellow on woollen, where the dye is made very strong. It requires an allum preparation and is managed the same in dyeing as has been mentioned for walnut or hickory bark.

USEFUL RECEIPTS.

To remove Iron Molds from Cotton or Linen.

Take an earthen vessel, pour into it boiling water, then spread the stained parts of your cloth over it, let it remain until well penetrated with the steam, then rub on the places sorrel juice mixed with salt until it is well soaked. Such cloths washed afterwards in common lye, will be made free from spots of mold.

To remove Carriage Wheel Grease from Woollen Cloth.

To effect this, the spots of grease must be first rubbed with fresh butter, then lay on two or three strips of blotting paper and apply a hot flat iron to it; this will entirely take out the spots.

To restore a Spoiled Wine.

Draw the wine off from its own lees and put it on the lees of good wine, then pulverise four or five nutmegs, with as many dry orange peels, add this mixture to the wine, stop the cask tight and let it ferment three weeks; after this time the wine will be found as good as ever.

To Clarify Wine.

Take 2 quarts of boiling milk, skim it well and while hot pour it into the cask.

A method to Soften Horn so that it may be cast in any shape.

Make a very strong lye with equal parts of quick lime and pearlash; rasp the horn and put the raspings in the lye; this mixture will soon become a paste, then add whatever color you choose, and it is ready for moulding in any shape. This composition should remain in the moulds two or three days, then boil them in a liquor made of allum and salt petre first; then boil them again in nut oil.

To make Ivory Soft.

Take 2 ounces of spirits of nitre, and 3 gills of soft spring water, mix them together and soak your ivory in it for 3 or 4 days, and it will be so soft as to receive impression from the fingers.

Method of Staining or Tinging Bones or Ivory, Red, (previously made soft.)

Boil the shreds of scarlet cloth in water; when it begins to boil throw in 4 ounces of ashes, made from Argol or the dregs of wine, which will extract the color—then throw in a little allum to clear it: then strain the liquor through a linen cloth. Steep the bone or ivory in this liquor. Should you wish white spots to be left on them cover the places with wax.

A method to take Oil Stains from Paper.

Books and manuscripts are sometimes defaced by accidental stains with oil; to remove such blemishes, burn sheep's bones and reduce them to a fine powder, lay a quantity of this powder on each side of the stain, place it between two sheets of white paper, submit it to a press for twelve hours. If the spots do not disappear, repeat the same.

To Boil Linseed Oil for Painting.

For one gallon of oil add one ounce of sugar of lead, and one ounce of white vitriol, which must be added only $\frac{1}{4}$ part at a time. Boil gently one hour, during which time it is to be stirred, then let it stand and settle and turn off only the clear part.

To Prepare Oil for Gilding.

Take linseed oil that has been boiled in the common way, put it in a glass bottle, hang it in the sun until it turns white and clear, which will be in about a week, in warm weather. Then mix it with some stone yellow, grind it fine and of the same thickness as common paint. Lay two coats in exactly the form you wish to have the gold lay: let it dry only until it has become a little sticky, then cut the leaf much in the form you wish to lay it, then take off the upper paper from the leaf, take the leaf with the other paper, then take off the paper and brush it over with a small ball made of cotton wool.

To make an Oil Varnish.

Take one quart of linseed oil, add 3 ounces of litharge, 1 ounce of burnt umber and half an ounce sugar of lead, boil it moderately until it settles clear, stirring it in the mean time. While cooling, add 1 ounce of white vitriol; when cold strain it off and put it in a glass bottle, stop it with a cork and hang it up with a wire hole in the cork; then let it hang until it is white and clear.

Apply this varnish to paint that is dry and let the sun come to it if convenient.

To make a Black Varnish.

Take gum-lac 4 ounces, sanderak and rosin 1 ounce each, pulverize them separately, dissolve the rosin over a fire in a sufficient quantity of spirit of wine, then add the sanderak to it; as soon as it is dissolved add the powder of gum-lac and stir it until it is well melted and mixed together. It is then to be strained while warm through a linen cloth. The black color is made by adding two drams of ivory black to every two ounces of the other.

Of the fine tortoise shell japan ground, produced by means of heat.

The best kind of tortoise shell ground produced by heat is not less valuable for its great hardness, and enduring to be made hotter than boiling water without damage, than for its beautiful appearance. It is to be made by means of a varnish prepared in the following manner.

"Take of good linseed oil one gallon, and of umber half a pound. Boil them together till the oil becomes very brown and thick; strain it then through a coarse cloth, and set it again to boil; in which state it must be continued till it acquires a pitchy consistence, when it will be fit for use."

Having prepared thus the varnish, clean well the iron or copper-plate, or other piece which is to be japanned; and then lay vermillion tempered with shell-lac varnish, or with drying oil diluted with oil of turpentine very thinly, on the places intended to imitate the more transparent parts of the tortoise shell. When the vermilion is dry, brush over the whole with the black varnish tempered to a due consistence with oil of turpentine; and when it is set and firm, put the work into a stove, where it may undergo a very strong heat, and must be continued a cousiderable time, if even three weeks or a month, it will be the better.

Of staining horn to imitate tortoise shell.

The horn to be stained must be first pressed into proper plates, or scales, or other flat form. The following mixture must then be prepared.

"Take of quicklime two parts, and of litharge one, and temper them to the consistence of a soft paste with soap lye."

Put this paste over all the parts of the horn, except such as are proper to be left transparent, in order to the greater resemblance of the tortoise shell. The horn must then remain thus covered with the paste till it be thoroughly dry: when the paste being brushed off, the horn will be found partly opake, and partly transparent, in the manner of tortoise shell, and when put over a foil, of the kind of latten called assidue, will be scarcely distinguishable from it. It requires some degree of fancy and judgment, to dispose of the paste in such a manner as to form a variety of transparent parts of different magnitude and figure, to look like the effect of nature; and it will be an improvement to add semitransparent parts: which may be done by mixing whiting with some of the paste to weaken its operation in particular places: by which spots of a reddish brown will be produced; that, if properly interspersed, especially on the edges of the dark parts, will greatly increase as well the beauty of the work, as its similitude with the real tortoise shell.

Of Gilding, proper for the Edges of Books and Paper.

There are several various methods, with respect to the cement used, by which the edges of books or paper may be gilt: as strong gum water, or insinglass size, or glover's size, may be employed: but as the gum water and weaker sizes, are apt to run beyond the edge and stick the leaves together, isinglass melted with the addition of some common proof spirit of wine, and a sixth part of honey or sugar candy is greatly preferable: but a third of bole armoniac well powdered must be added.

The following composition has been likewise approved of for this purpose.

"Take bole armoniac and sugar candy well powdered, each equal parts; mix them with whites of eggs beaten to an oily consistence, and the cement will be fit for use."

In order to the using any of these cements, the paper, whether it be in quires or books, should be well cut, and polished on the edges to be gilt; and then strongly screwed down by the press; in which state, it is to be brushed over, first with a little of the cement without the sugar candy, or the bole; and when that is dry, either with the cement above given, or any other solution of gum or size with the proper proportion of the bole: after which it may be suffered to dry, and then water polished by rubbing it with a fine linen rag slightly moistened. It is then in a state fit for receiving the gold, only it must be again gently moistened at that time, and the leaves may then be laid on, being cut according to the breadth they are to cover, and pressed closely down by a cotton ball, and after the gilding is thoroughly dry and firm, it may be polished in the manner of the foregoing kinds.

Of Staining Wood of Mahogany Color.

Mahogony color is the most useful of any stain for wood (especially since the fineering with different colors is out of fashion) as it is much practised at present for chairs and other furniture made in imitation of mahogony; which when well managed, may be brought to have a very near resemblance.

This stain may be of different hues, as the natural wood varies greatly, being of all the intermediate tints between the red brown and purple brown, according to the age, or sometimes the original nature of different pieces.

For the light red brown, use a decoction of madder, or fustic wood, ground in water; the proportion may be half a pound of madder and a quarter of a pound of fustic, to a gallon: or in default of fustic, an ounce of the yellow berries may be used. This must be brushed over the wood to be stained, while boiling hot, till the due color be obtained; and, if the wood be kindly grained, it will have greatly the appearance of new mahogany.

The same effect, nearly, may be produced by the tincture of dragon's blood and turmeric root, in spirit of wine: by increasing or diminishing the proportion of each of which ingredients, the brown stain may be varied to a more red or yellow cast at pleasure. This succeeds better upon wood which has already some tinge of brown, than upon whiter.

For the dark mahogony, take the infusion of madder made as above, except the exchanging the fustic for 2 ounces of logwood, and when the wood to be stained has been several times brushed over, and is again dry, it must be slightly brushed over with water in which pearlashes have been dissolved, in the proportion of about a quarter of an ounce to a quart.

Any stains of the intermediate colors may be made by mixing these ingredients, or varying the proportion of them.

Where these stains are used for better kind of work, the wood should be afterwards varnished with three or four coats of seed-lac varnish; but for coarse work, the varnish of resin and seed-lac may be emplyed, or they may be only well rubbed over with drying oil.

Of Staining Wood Red.

For a bright red stain for wood, make a strong infusion of Brazil in stale urine, or water impregnated with pearlashes in the proportion of an ounce to a gallon; to a gallon of either of which, the proportion of Brazil wood must be a pound: which being put to them, they must stand together two or three days, often stirring the mixture. With this infusion strained and made boiling hot, brush over the wood to be stained, till it appears strongly colored; then, while yet wet, brush it over with allum water made in the proportion of two ounces of allum to a quart of water.

For a less bright red, dissolve an ounce of dragon's blood in a pint of spirit of wine, and brush over the wood with the tincture, till the stain appears to be as strong as desired.

For a pink or rose red, add to a gallon of the above infusion of Brazilwood two additional ounces of the pearlashes and use it as was before directed; but it is necessary, in this case, to brush the wood over often with the allum water. By increasing the proportion of pearlashes, the red may be rendered yet paler; but it is proper, when more than this quantity is added, to make the allum water stronger.

Of Isinglass Glue.

"Isinglass glue is made by dissolving beaten insinglass in water; and, having strained it through a coarse linen cloth, evaporating it again to such a consistence, that being cold the glue will be perfectly hard and dry."

A great improvement may be made in this glue by adding spirit of wine or brandy to it after it is strained, and then renewing the evaporation till it gain the due consistence. Some soak the isinglass in the spirit or brandy for some time before it is dissolved, in order to make the glue, and add no water, but let the spirit supply the place of it.

This isinglass glue is far preferable to common glue for nicer purposes; being much stronger and less liable to be softened either by heat or moisture.

Preparation of a very strong Compound Glue.

"Take common glue in very small or thin bits, and isinglass glue, and infuse them in as much spirit of wine as will cover them, for at least twenty-four hours. Then melt the whole together, and while they are over the fire, add as much powdered chalk as will render them an opake white."

Composition of common black ink.

"Take one gallon of soft water, and pour it boiling hot on one pound of powdered galls, put into a proper vessel. Stop the mouth of the vessel, and set it in the sun in summer, or in winter where it may be warmed by any fire, and let it stand two or three days. Add then half a pound of green vitriol powdered; and having stirred the mixture well together with a wooden spatula, let it stand again for two or three days, repeating the stirring; when add further to it five ounces of gum Arabic dissolved in a quart of boiling water, and lastly two ounces of allum: after which the ink should be strained through a coarse linen cloth for use."

Preparation of red writing ink.

"Take of the raspings of Brazil wood a quarter of a pound, and infuse them two or three days in vinegar, which should be colorless when it can be so procured. Boil the infusion then an hour over a gentle fire, and afterwards filter it, while hot, through paper laid in an earthen cullender. Put it again over the fire, and dissolve in it, first half an ounce of gum Arabic; and afterwards of allum and white sugar, each half an ounce.

Care should be taken that the Brazil wood be not adulterated with the Braziletto or Campeachy (commonly called peachy) wood; which is mostly the case, when it is ground: and though a very detrimental fraud in all instances of the application of Brazil wood to the forming bright red colors, cannot yet be perceived after the mixture of the raspings, but by trial in using them; it is therefore much the best way, when it is wanted for purposes like this, to procure the true Brazil wood in pieces, and to scrape it with a knife, or rasp it with a very bright file, (but all rust of iron must be carefully avoided) by which means all possibility of sophistication is of course prevented.

Red ink may likewise be prepared, by the above process, of white wine instead of vinegar; but it should be sour, or disposed to be so, otherwise, a third or fourth of vinegar should be added, in order to its taking the stronger tincture from the wood. Small beer has been sometimes used for the same purpose; but the ink will not be so bright, and when it is used vinegar should be added, and the quantity of gum Arabic diminished, and the sugar wholly omitted.

Preparation of red ink from vermilion.

"Take the glair of four eggs, a tea spoonful of white sugar or sugar candy beaten to powder, and as much spirit of wine; and beat them together till they be of the consistence of oil. Then add such a proportion of vermilion as will produce a red color, sufficiently strong, and keep the mixture in a small phial or well stopped ink bottle for use. The composition should be well shaken together before it be used."

Instead of the glair of eggs, gum water is frequently used, but thin size made of isinglass with a little honey, is much better for the purpose.

Composition of the best hard red sealing wax.

"Take of shell-lac, well powdered, two parts, of resin and vermillion powered also each one part. Mix them well together, and melt them over a gentle fire; and when the ingredients seem thoroughly incorporated, work the wax into sticks. Where shell-lac cannot be procured, seed-lac may be substituted for it."

The quantity of vermillion, which is much the dearest ingredient, may be diminished without any injury to the sealing wax, where it is not required to be of the highest and brightest red color: and the resin should be of the whitest kind, as that improves the effect of the vermillion.

Care should be taken not to use too strong a fire in melting the ingredients; and to remove them out of the heat, as soon as they be well commixed; for if any evaporation of the more volatile parts of the shell or red lac, or resin, be suffered, the wax is rendered proportionably brittle.

A CATALOGUE OF SELECTED DOVER BOOKS
IN ALL FIELDS OF INTEREST

A CATALOGUE OF SELECTED DOVER BOOKS IN ALL FIELDS OF INTEREST

CREATIVE LITHOGRAPHY AND HOW TO DO IT, Grant Arnold. Lithography as art form: working directly on stone, transfer of drawings, lithotint, mezzotint, color printing; also metal plates. Detailed, thorough. 27 illustrations. 214pp.
21208-4 Pa. $3.00

DESIGN MOTIFS OF ANCIENT MEXICO, Jorge Enciso. Vigorous, powerful ceramic stamp impressions — Maya, Aztec, Toltec, Olmec. Serpents, gods, priests, dancers, etc. 153pp. 6⅛ x 9¼. 20084-1 Pa. $2.50

AMERICAN INDIAN DESIGN AND DECORATION, Leroy Appleton. Full text, plus more than 700 precise drawings of Inca, Maya, Aztec, Pueblo, Plains, NW Coast basketry, sculpture, painting, pottery, sand paintings, metal, etc. 4 plates in color. 279pp. 8⅜ x 11¼. 22704-9 Pa. $4.50

CHINESE LATTICE DESIGNS, Daniel S. Dye. Incredibly beautiful geometric designs: circles, voluted, simple dissections, etc. Inexhaustible source of ideas, motifs. 1239 illustrations. 469pp. 6⅛ x 9¼. 23096-1 Pa. $5.00

JAPANESE DESIGN MOTIFS, Matsuya Co. Mon, or heraldic designs. Over 4000 typical, beautiful designs: birds, animals, flowers, swords, fans, geometric; all beautifully stylized. 213pp. 11⅜ x 8¼. 22874-6 Pa. $5.00

PERSPECTIVE, Jan Vredeman de Vries. 73 perspective plates from 1604 edition; buildings, townscapes, stairways, fantastic scenes. Remarkable for beauty, surrealistic atmosphere; real eye-catchers. Introduction by Adolf Placzek. 74pp. 11⅜ x 8¼. 20186-4 Pa. $2.75

EARLY AMERICAN DESIGN MOTIFS, Suzanne E. Chapman. 497 motifs, designs, from painting on wood, ceramics, appliqué, glassware, samplers, metal work, etc. Florals, landscapes, birds and animals, geometrics, letters, etc. Inexhaustible. Enlarged edition. 138pp. 8⅜ x 11¼. 22985-8 Pa. $3.50
23084-8 Clothbd. $7.95

VICTORIAN STENCILS FOR DESIGN AND DECORATION, edited by E.V. Gillon, Jr. 113 wonderful ornate Victorian pieces from German sources; florals, geometrics; borders, corner pieces; bird motifs, etc. 64pp. 9⅜ x 12¼. 21995-X Pa. $2.75

ART NOUVEAU: AN ANTHOLOGY OF DESIGN AND ILLUSTRATION FROM THE STUDIO, edited by E.V. Gillon, Jr. Graphic arts: book jackets, posters, engravings, illustrations, decorations; Crane, Beardsley, Bradley and many others. Inexhaustible. 92pp. 8⅛ x 11. 22388-4 Pa. $2.50

ORIGINAL ART DECO DESIGNS, William Rowe. First-rate, highly imaginative modern Art Deco frames, borders, compositions, alphabets, florals, insectals, Wurlitzer-types, etc. Much finest modern Art Deco. 80 plates, 8 in color. 8⅜ x 11¼. 22567-4 Pa. $3.00

HANDBOOK OF DESIGNS AND DEVICES, Clarence P. Hornung. Over 1800 basic geometric designs based on circle, triangle, square, scroll, cross, etc. Largest such collection in existence. 261pp. 20125-2 Pa. $2.50

150 Masterpieces of Drawing, edited by Anthony Toney. 150 plates, early 15th century to end of 18th century; Rembrandt, Michelangelo, Dürer, Fragonard, Watteau, Wouwerman, many others. 150pp. 8³/8 x 11¼. 21032-4 Pa. $3.50

The Golden Age of the Poster, Hayward and Blanche Cirker. 70 extraordinary posters in full colors, from Maîtres de l'Affiche, Mucha, Lautrec, Bradley, Cheret, Beardsley, many others. 9³/8 x 12¼. 22753-7 Pa. $4.95
21718-3 Clothbd. $7.95

Simplicissimus, selection, translations and text by Stanley Appelbaum. 180 satirical drawings, 16 in full color, from the famous German weekly magazine in the years 1896 to 1926. 24 artists included: Grosz, Kley, Pascin, Kubin, Kollwitz, plus Heine, Thöny, Bruno Paul, others. 172pp. 8½ x 12¼. 23098-8 Pa. $5.00
23099-6 Clothbd. $10.00

The Early Work of Aubrey Beardsley, Aubrey Beardsley. 157 plates, 2 in color: Manon Lescaut, Madame Bovary, Morte d'Arthur, Salome, other. Introduction by H. Marillier. 175pp. 8½ x 11. 21816-3 Pa. $3.50

The Later Work of Aubrey Beardsley, Aubrey Beardsley. Exotic masterpieces of full maturity: Venus and Tannhäuser, Lysistrata, Rape of the Lock, Volpone, Savoy material, etc. 174 plates, 2 in color. 176pp. 8½ x 11. 21817-1 Pa. $4.00

Drawings of William Blake, William Blake. 92 plates from Book of Job, Divine Comedy, Paradise Lost, visionary heads, mythological figures, Laocoön, etc. Selection, introduction, commentary by Sir Geoffrey Keynes. 178pp. 8½ x 11. 22303-5 Pa. $3.50

London: A Pilgrimage, Gustave Doré, Blanchard Jerrold. Squalor, riches, misery, beauty of mid-Victorian metropolis; 55 wonderful plates, 125 other illustrations, full social, cultural text by Jerrold. 191pp. of text. 8¹/8 x 11.
22306-X Pa. $5.00

The Complete Woodcuts of Albrecht Dürer, edited by Dr. W. Kurth. 346 in all: Old Testament, St. Jerome, Passion, Life of Virgin, Apocalypse, many others. Introduction by Campbell Dodgson. 285pp. 8½ x 12¼. 21097-9 Pa. $6.00

The Disasters of War, Francisco Goya. 83 etchings record horrors of Napoleonic wars in Spain and war in general. Reprint of 1st edition, plus 3 additional plates. Introduction by Philip Hofer. 97pp. 9³/8 x 8¼. 21872-4 Pa. $3.00

Engravings of Hogarth, William Hogarth. 101 of Hogarth's greatest works: Rake's Progress, Harlot's Progress, Illustrations for Hudibras, Midnight Modern Conversation, Before and After, Beer Street and Gin Lane, many more. Full commentary. 256pp. 11 x 14. 22479-1 Pa. $7.00
23023-6 Clothbd. $13.50

Primitive Art, Franz Boas. Great anthropologist on ceramics, textiles, wood, stone, metal, etc.; patterns, technology, symbols, styles. All areas, but fullest on Northwest Coast Indians. 350 illustrations. 378pp. 20025-6 Pa. $3.50

MOTHER GOOSE'S MELODIES. Facsimile of fabulously rare Munroe and Francis "copyright 1833" Boston edition. Familiar and unusual rhymes, wonderful old woodcut illustrations. Edited by E.F. Bleiler. 128pp. 4½ x 6⅜. 22577-1 Pa. $1.00

MOTHER GOOSE IN HIEROGLYPHICS. Favorite nursery rhymes presented in rebus form for children. Fascinating 1849 edition reproduced in toto, with key. Introduction by E.F. Bleiler. About 400 woodcuts. 64pp. 6⅞ x 5¼. 20745-5 Pa. $1.00

PETER PIPER'S PRACTICAL PRINCIPLES OF PLAIN & PERFECT PRONUNCIATION. Alliterative jingles and tongue-twisters. Reproduction in full of 1830 first American edition. 25 spirited woodcuts. 32pp. 4½ x 6⅜. 22560-7 Pa. $1.00

MARMADUKE MULTIPLY'S MERRY METHOD OF MAKING MINOR MATHEMATICIANS. Fellow to Peter Piper, it teaches multiplication table by catchy rhymes and woodcuts. 1841 Munroe & Francis edition. Edited by E.F. Bleiler. 103pp. 4⅝ x 6.
22773-1 Pa. $1.25
20171-6 Clothbd. $3.00

THE NIGHT BEFORE CHRISTMAS, Clement Moore. Full text, and woodcuts from original 1848 book. Also critical, historical material. 19 illustrations. 40pp. 4⅝ x 6. 22797-9 Pa. $1.00

THE KING OF THE GOLDEN RIVER, John Ruskin. Victorian children's classic of three brothers, their attempts to reach the Golden River, what becomes of them. Facsimile of original 1889 edition. 22 illustrations. 56pp. 4⅝ x 6⅜.
20066-3 Pa. $1.25

DREAMS OF THE RAREBIT FIEND, Winsor McCay. Pioneer cartoon strip, unexcelled for beauty, imagination, in 60 full sequences. Incredible technical virtuosity, wonderful visual wit. Historical introduction. 62pp. 8⅜ x 11¼. 21347-1 Pa. $2.50

THE KATZENJAMMER KIDS, Rudolf Dirks. In full color, 14 strips from 1906-7; full of imagination, characteristic humor. Classic of great historical importance. Introduction by August Derleth. 32pp. 9¼ x 12¼. 23005-8 Pa. $2.00

LITTLE ORPHAN ANNIE AND LITTLE ORPHAN ANNIE IN COSMIC CITY, Harold Gray. Two great sequences from the early strips: our curly-haired heroine defends the Warbucks' financial empire and, then, takes on meanie Phineas P. Pinchpenny. Leapin' lizards! 178pp. 6⅛ x 8⅜. 23107-0 Pa. $2.00

WHEN A FELLER NEEDS A FRIEND, Clare Briggs. 122 cartoons by one of the greatest newspaper cartoonists of the early 20th century — about growing up, making a living, family life, daily frustrations and occasional triumphs. 121pp. 8½ x 9½.
23148-8 Pa. $2.50

THE BEST OF GLUYAS WILLIAMS. 100 drawings by one of America's finest cartoonists: The Day a Cake of Ivory Soap Sank at Proctor & Gamble's, At the Life Insurance Agents' Banquet, and many other gems from the 20's and 30's. 118pp. 8⅜ x 11¼. 22737-5 Pa. $2.50

THE BEST DR. THORNDYKE DETECTIVE STORIES, R. Austin Freeman. The Case of Oscar Brodski, The Moabite Cipher, and 5 other favorites featuring the great scientific detective, plus his long-believed-lost first adventure — 31 New Inn — reprinted here for the first time. Edited by E.F. Bleiler. USO 20388-3 Pa. $3.00

BEST "THINKING MACHINE" DETECTIVE STORIES, Jacques Futrelle. The Problem of Cell 13 and 11 other stories about Prof. Augustus S.F.X. Van Dusen, including two "lost" stories. First reprinting of several. Edited by E.F. Bleiler. 241pp. 20537-1 Pa. $3.00

UNCLE SILAS, J. Sheridan LeFanu. Victorian Gothic mystery novel, considered by many best of period, even better than Collins or Dickens. Wonderful psychological terror. Introduction by Frederick Shroyer. 436pp. 21715-9 Pa. $4.00

BEST DR. POGGIOLI DETECTIVE STORIES, T.S. Stribling. 15 best stories from EQMM and The Saint offer new adventures in Mexico, Florida, Tennessee hills as Poggioli unravels mysteries and combats Count Jalacki. 217pp. 23227-1 Pa. $3.00

EIGHT DIME NOVELS, selected with an introduction by E.F. Bleiler. Adventures of Old King Brady, Frank James, Nick Carter, Deadwood Dick, Buffalo Bill, The Steam Man, Frank Merriwell, and Horatio Alger — 1877 to 1905. Important, entertaining popular literature in facsimile reprint, with original covers. 190pp. 9 x 12. 22975-0 Pa. $3.50

ALICE'S ADVENTURES UNDER GROUND, Lewis Carroll. Facsimile of ms. Carroll gave Alice Liddell in 1864. Different in many ways from final Alice. Handlettered, illustrated by Carroll. Introduction by Martin Gardner. 128pp. 21482-6 Pa. $1.50

ALICE IN WONDERLAND COLORING BOOK, Lewis Carroll. Pictures by John Tenniel. Large-size versions of the famous illustrations of Alice, Cheshire Cat, Mad Hatter and all the others, waiting for your crayons. Abridged text. 36 illustrations. 64pp. 8¼ x 11. 22853-3 Pa. $1.50

AVENTURES D'ALICE AU PAYS DES MERVEILLES, Lewis Carroll. Bué's translation of "Alice" into French, supervised by Carroll himself. Novel way to learn language. (No English text.) 42 Tenniel illustrations. 196pp. 22836-3 Pa. $2.50

MYTHS AND FOLK TALES OF IRELAND, Jeremiah Curtin. 11 stories that are Irish versions of European fairy tales and 9 stories from the Fenian cycle — 20 tales of legend and magic that comprise an essential work in the history of folklore. 256pp. 22430-9 Pa. $3.00

EAST O' THE SUN AND WEST O' THE MOON, George W. Dasent. Only full edition of favorite, wonderful Norwegian fairytales — Why the Sea is Salt, Boots and the Troll, etc. — with 77 illustrations by Kittelsen & Werenskiöld. 418pp. 22521-6 Pa. $4.00

PERRAULT'S FAIRY TALES, Charles Perrault and Gustave Doré. Original versions of Cinderella, Sleeping Beauty, Little Red Riding Hood, etc. in best translation, with 34 wonderful illustrations by Gustave Doré. 117pp. 8⅛ x 11. 22311-6 Pa. $2.50

EARLY NEW ENGLAND GRAVESTONE RUBBINGS, Edmund V. Gillon, Jr. 43 photographs, 226 rubbings show heavily symbolic, macabre, sometimes humorous primitive American art. Up to early 19th century. 207pp. 8$^{3}/_{8}$ x 11$^{1}/_{4}$.
21380-3 Pa. $4.00

L.J.M. DAGUERRE: THE HISTORY OF THE DIORAMA AND THE DAGUERREOTYPE, Helmut and Alison Gernsheim. Definitive account. Early history, life and work of Daguerre; discovery of daguerreotype process; diffusion abroad; other early photography. 124 illustrations. 226pp. 6$^{1}/_{6}$ x 9$^{1}/_{4}$. 22290-X Pa. $4.00

PHOTOGRAPHY AND THE AMERICAN SCENE, Robert Taft. The basic book on American photography as art, recording form, 1839-1889. Development, influence on society, great photographers, types (portraits, war, frontier, etc.), whatever else needed. Inexhaustible. Illustrated with 322 early photos, daguerreotypes, tintypes, stereo slides, etc. 546pp. 6$^{1}/_{8}$ x 9$^{1}/_{4}$. 21201-7 Pa. $5.95

PHOTOGRAPHIC SKETCHBOOK OF THE CIVIL WAR, Alexander Gardner. Reproduction of 1866 volume with 100 on-the-field photographs: Manassas, Lincoln on battlefield, slave pens, etc. Introduction by E.F. Bleiler. 224pp. 10$^{3}/_{4}$ x 9.
22731-6 Pa. $5.00

THE MOVIES: A PICTURE QUIZ BOOK, Stanley Appelbaum & Hayward Cirker. Match stars with their movies, name actors and actresses, test your movie skill with 241 stills from 236 great movies, 1902-1959. Indexes of performers and films. 128pp. 8$^{3}/_{8}$ x 9$^{1}/_{4}$. 20222-4 Pa. $2.50

THE TALKIES, Richard Griffith. Anthology of features, articles from Photoplay, 1928-1940, reproduced complete. Stars, famous movies, technical features, fabulous ads, etc.; Garbo, Chaplin, King Kong, Lubitsch, etc. 4 color plates, scores of illustrations. 327pp. 8$^{3}/_{8}$ x 11$^{1}/_{4}$. 22762-6 Pa. $6.95

THE MOVIE MUSICAL FROM VITAPHONE TO "42ND STREET," edited by Miles Kreuger. Relive the rise of the movie musical as reported in the pages of Photoplay magazine (1926-1933): every movie review, cast list, ad, and record review; every significant feature article, production still, biography, forecast, and gossip story. Profusely illustrated. 367pp. 8$^{3}/_{8}$ x 11$^{1}/_{4}$. 23154-2 Pa. $6.95

JOHANN SEBASTIAN BACH, Philipp Spitta. Great classic of biography, musical commentary, with hundreds of pieces analyzed. Also good for Bach's contemporaries. 450 musical examples. Total of 1799pp.
EUK 22278-0, 22279-9 Clothbd., Two vol. set $25.00

BEETHOVEN AND HIS NINE SYMPHONIES, Sir George Grove. Thorough history, analysis, commentary on symphonies and some related pieces. For either beginner or advanced student. 436 musical passages. 407pp. 20334-4 Pa. $4.00

MOZART AND HIS PIANO CONCERTOS, Cuthbert Girdlestone. The only full-length study. Detailed analyses of all 21 concertos, sources; 417 musical examples. 509pp. 21271-8 Pa. $4.50

THE FITZWILLIAM VIRGINAL BOOK, edited by J. Fuller Maitland, W.B. Squire. Famous early 17th century collection of keyboard music, 300 works by Morley, Byrd, Bull, Gibbons, etc. Modern notation. Total of 938pp. 8³/₈ x 11.
ECE 21068-5, 21069-3 Pa., Two vol. set $14.00

COMPLETE STRING QUARTETS, Wolfgang A. Mozart. Breitkopf and Härtel edition. All 23 string quartets plus alternate slow movement to K156. Study score. 277pp. 9³/₈ x 12¼. 22372-8 Pa. $6.00

COMPLETE SONG CYCLES, Franz Schubert. Complete piano, vocal music of Die Schöne Müllerin, Die Winterreise, Schwanengesang. Also Drinker English singing translations. Breitkopf and Härtel edition. 217pp. 9³/₈ x 12¼.
22649-2 Pa. $4.50

THE COMPLETE PRELUDES AND ETUDES FOR PIANOFORTE SOLO, Alexander Scriabin. All the preludes and etudes including many perfectly spun miniatures. Edited by K.N. Igumnov and Y.I. Mil'shteyn. 250pp. 9 x 12. 22919-X Pa. $5.00

TRISTAN UND ISOLDE, Richard Wagner. Full orchestral score with complete instrumentation. Do not confuse with piano reduction. Commentary by Felix Mottl, great Wagnerian conductor and scholar. Study score. 655pp. 8¹/₈ x 11.
22915-7 Pa. $10.00

FAVORITE SONGS OF THE NINETIES, ed. Robert Fremont. Full reproduction, including covers, of 88 favorites: Ta-Ra-Ra-Boom-De-Aye, The Band Played On, Bird in a Gilded Cage, Under the Bamboo Tree, After the Ball, etc. 401pp. 9 x 12.
EBE 21536-9 Pa. $6.95

SOUSA'S GREAT MARCHES IN PIANO TRANSCRIPTION: ORIGINAL SHEET MUSIC OF 23 WORKS, John Philip Sousa. Selected by Lester S. Levy. Playing edition includes: The Stars and Stripes Forever, The Thunderer, The Gladiator, King Cotton, Washington Post, much more. 24 illustrations. 111pp. 9 x 12.
USO 23132-1 Pa. $3.50

CLASSIC PIANO RAGS, selected with an introduction by Rudi Blesh. Best ragtime music (1897-1922) by Scott Joplin, James Scott, Joseph F. Lamb, Tom Turpin, 9 others. Printed from best original sheet music, plus covers. 364pp. 9 x 12.
EBE 20469-3 Pa. $6.95

ANALYSIS OF CHINESE CHARACTERS, C.D. Wilder, J.H. Ingram. 1000 most important characters analyzed according to primitives, phonetics, historical development. Traditional method offers mnemonic aid to beginner, intermediate student of Chinese, Japanese. 365pp. 23045-7 Pa. $4.00

MODERN CHINESE: A BASIC COURSE, Faculty of Peking University. Self study, classroom course in modern Mandarin. Records contain phonetics, vocabulary, sentences, lessons. 249 page book contains all recorded text, translations, grammar, vocabulary, exercises. Best course on market. 3 12" 33⅓ monaural records, book, album. 98832-5 Set $12.50

CONSTRUCTION OF AMERICAN FURNITURE TREASURES, Lester Margon. 344 detail drawings, complete text on constructing exact reproductions of 38 early American masterpieces: Hepplewhite sideboard, Duncan Phyfe drop-leaf table, mantel clock, gate-leg dining table, Pa. German cupboard, more. 38 plates. 54 photographs. 168pp. 8⅜ x 11¼. 23056-2 Pa. $4.00

JEWELRY MAKING AND DESIGN, Augustus F. Rose, Antonio Cirino. Professional secrets revealed in thorough, practical guide: tools, materials, processes; rings, brooches, chains, cast pieces, enamelling, setting stones, etc. Do not confuse with skimpy introductions: beginner can use, professional can learn from it. Over 200 illustrations. 306pp. 21750-7 Pa. $3.00

METALWORK AND ENAMELLING, Herbert Maryon. Generally coneeded best all-around book. Countless trade secrets: materials, tools, soldering, filigree, setting, inlay, niello, repoussé, casting, polishing, etc. For beginner or expert. Author was foremost British expert. 330 illustrations. 335pp. 22702-2 Pa. $3.50

WEAVING WITH FOOT-POWER LOOMS, Edward F. Worst. Setting up a loom, beginning to weave, constructing equipment, using dyes, more, plus over 285 drafts of traditional patterns including Colonial and Swedish weaves. More than 200 other figures. For beginning and advanced. 275pp. 8¾ x 6⅜. 23064-3 Pa. $4.00

WEAVING A NAVAJO BLANKET, Gladys A. Reichard. Foremost anthropologist studied under Navajo women, reveals every step in process from wool, dyeing, spinning, setting up loom, designing, weaving. Much history, symbolism. With this book you could make one yourself. 97 illustrations. 222pp. 22992-0 Pa. $3.00

NATURAL DYES AND HOME DYEING, Rita J. Adrosko. Use natural ingredients: bark, flowers, leaves, lichens, insects etc. Over 135 specific recipes from historical sources for cotton, wool, other fabrics. Genuine premodern handicrafts. 12 illustrations. 160pp. 22688-3 Pa. $2.00

THE HAND DECORATION OF FABRICS, Francis J. Kafka. Outstanding, profusely illustrated guide to stenciling, batik, block printing, tie dyeing, freehand painting, silk screen printing, and novelty decoration. 356 illustrations. 198pp. 6 x 9. 21401-X Pa. $3.00

THOMAS NAST: CARTOONS AND ILLUSTRATIONS, with text by Thomas Nast St. Hill. Father of American political cartooning. Cartoons that destroyed Tweed Ring; inflation, free love, church and state; original Republican elephant and Democratic donkey; Santa Claus; more. 117 illustrations. 146pp. 9 x 12. 22983-1 Pa. $4.00
23067-8 Clothbd. $8.50

FREDERIC REMINGTON: 173 DRAWINGS AND ILLUSTRATIONS. Most famous of the Western artists, most responsible for our myths about the American West in its untamed days. Complete reprinting of *Drawings of Frederic Remington* (1897), plus other selections. 4 additional drawings in color on covers. 140pp. 9 x 12. 20714-5 Pa. $3.95

HOW TO SOLVE CHESS PROBLEMS, Kenneth S. Howard. Practical suggestions on problem solving for very beginners. 58 two-move problems, 46 3-movers, 8 4-movers for practice, plus hints. 171pp. 20748-X Pa. $2.00

A GUIDE TO FAIRY CHESS, Anthony Dickins. 3-D chess, 4-D chess, chess on a cylindrical board, reflecting pieces that bounce off edges, cooperative chess, retrograde chess, maximummers, much more. Most based on work of great Dawson. Full handbook, 100 problems. 66pp. 7⅞ x 10¾. 22687-5 Pa. $2.00

WIN AT BACKGAMMON, Millard Hopper. Best opening moves, running game, blocking game, back game, tables of odds, etc. Hopper makes the game clear enough for anyone to play, and win. 43 diagrams. 111pp. 22894-0 Pa. $1.50

BIDDING A BRIDGE HAND, Terence Reese. Master player "thinks out loud" the binding of 75 hands that defy point count systems. Organized by bidding problem—no-fit situations, overbidding, underbidding, cueing your defense, etc. 254pp. EBE 22830-4 Pa. $2.50

THE PRECISION BIDDING SYSTEM IN BRIDGE, C.C. Wei, edited by Alan Truscott. Inventor of precision bidding presents average hands and hands from actual play, including games from 1969 Bermuda Bowl where system emerged. 114 exercises. 116pp. 21171-1 Pa. $1.75

LEARN MAGIC, Henry Hay. 20 simple, easy-to-follow lessons on magic for the new magician: illusions, card tricks, silks, sleights of hand, coin manipulations, escapes, and more —all with a minimum amount of equipment. Final chapter explains the great stage illusions. 92 illustrations. 285pp. 21238-6 Pa. $2.95

THE NEW MAGICIAN'S MANUAL, Walter B. Gibson. Step-by-step instructions and clear illustrations guide the novice in mastering 36 tricks; much equipment supplied on 16 pages of cut-out materials. 36 additional tricks. 64 illustrations. 159pp. 6⅝ x 10. 23113-5 Pa. $3.00

PROFESSIONAL MAGIC FOR AMATEURS, Walter B. Gibson. 50 easy, effective tricks used by professionals —cards, string, tumblers, handkerchiefs, mental magic, etc. 63 illustrations. 223pp. 23012-0 Pa. $2.50

CARD MANIPULATIONS, Jean Hugard. Very rich collection of manipulations; has taught thousands of fine magicians tricks that are really workable, eye-catching. Easily followed, serious work. Over 200 illustrations. 163pp. 20539-8 Pa. $2.00

ABBOTT'S ENCYCLOPEDIA OF ROPE TRICKS FOR MAGICIANS, Stewart James. Complete reference book for amateur and professional magicians containing more than 150 tricks involving knots, penetrations, cut and restored rope, etc. 510 illustrations. Reprint of 3rd edition. 400pp. 23206-9 Pa. $3.50

THE SECRETS OF HOUDINI, J.C. Cannell. Classic study of Houdini's incredible magic, exposing closely-kept professional secrets and revealing, in general terms, the whole art of stage magic. 67 illustrations. 279pp. 22913-0 Pa. $2.50

THE MAGIC MOVING PICTURE BOOK, Bliss, Sands & Co. The pictures in this book move! Volcanoes erupt, a house burns, a serpentine dancer wiggles her way through a number. By using a specially ruled acetate screen provided, you can obtain these and 15 other startling effects. Originally "The Motograph Moving Picture Book." 32pp. 8¼ x 11. 23224-7 Pa. $1.75

STRING FIGURES AND HOW TO MAKE THEM, Caroline F. Jayne. Fullest, clearest instructions on string figures from around world: Eskimo, Navajo, Lapp, Europe, more. Cats cradle, moving spear, lightning, stars. Introduction by A.C. Haddon. 950 illustrations. 407pp. 20152-X Pa. $3.00

PAPER FOLDING FOR BEGINNERS, William D. Murray and Francis J. Rigney. Clearest book on market for making origami sail boats, roosters, frogs that move legs, cups, bonbon boxes. 40 projects. More than 275 illustrations. Photographs. 94pp. 20713-7 Pa. $1.25

INDIAN SIGN LANGUAGE, William Tomkins. Over 525 signs developed by Sioux, Blackfoot, Cheyenne, Arapahoe and other tribes. Written instructions and diagrams: how to make words, construct sentences. Also 290 pictographs of Sioux and Ojibway tribes. 111pp. 6⅛ x 9¼. 22029-X Pa. $1.50

BOOMERANGS: HOW TO MAKE AND THROW THEM, Bernard S. Mason. Easy to make and throw, dozens of designs: cross-stick, pinwheel, boomabird, tumblestick, Australian curved stick boomerang. Complete throwing instructions. All safe. 99pp. 23028-7 Pa. $1.50

25 KITES THAT FLY, Leslie Hunt. Full, easy to follow instructions for kites made from inexpensive materials. Many novelties. Reeling, raising, designing your own. 70 illustrations. 110pp. 22550-X Pa. $1.25

TRICKS AND GAMES ON THE POOL TABLE, Fred Herrmann. 79 tricks and games, some solitaires, some for 2 or more players, some competitive; mystifying shots and throws, unusual carom, tricks involving cork, coins, a hat, more. 77 figures. 95pp. 21814-7 Pa. $1.25

WOODCRAFT AND CAMPING, Bernard S. Mason. How to make a quick emergency shelter, select woods that will burn immediately, make do with limited supplies, etc. Also making many things out of wood, rawhide, bark, at camp. Formerly titled Woodcraft. 295 illustrations. 580pp. 21951-8 Pa. $4.00

AN INTRODUCTION TO CHESS MOVES AND TACTICS SIMPLY EXPLAINED, Leonard Barden. Informal intermediate introduction: reasons for moves, tactics, openings, traps, positional play, endgame. Isolates patterns. 102pp. USO 21210-6 Pa. $1.35

LASKER'S MANUAL OF CHESS, Dr. Emanuel Lasker. Great world champion offers very thorough coverage of all aspects of chess. Combinations, position play, openings, endgame, aesthetics of chess, philosophy of struggle, much more. Filled with analyzed games. 390pp. 20640-8 Pa. $3.50

SLEEPING BEAUTY, illustrated by Arthur Rackham. Perhaps the fullest, most delightful version ever, told by C.S. Evans. Rackham's best work. 49 illustrations. 110pp. 7⅞ x 10¾. 22756-1 Pa. $2.00

THE WONDERFUL WIZARD OF OZ, L. Frank Baum. Facsimile in full color of America's finest children's classic. Introduction by Martin Gardner. 143 illustrations by W.W. Denslow. 267pp. 20691-2 Pa. $2.50

GOOPS AND HOW TO BE THEM, Gelett Burgess. Classic tongue-in-cheek masquerading as etiquette book. 87 verses, 170 cartoons as Goops demonstrate virtues of table manners, neatness, courtesy, more. 88pp. 6½ x 9¼. 22233-0 Pa. $1.50

THE BROWNIES, THEIR BOOK, Palmer Cox. Small as mice, cunning as foxes, exuberant, mischievous, Brownies go to zoo, toy shop, seashore, circus, more. 24 verse adventures. 266 illustrations. 144pp. 6⅝ x 9¼. 21265-3 Pa. $1.75

BILLY WHISKERS: THE AUTOBIOGRAPHY OF A GOAT, Frances Trego Montgomery. Escapades of that rambunctious goat. Favorite from turn of the century America. 24 illustrations. 259pp. 22345-0 Pa. $2.75

THE ROCKET BOOK, Peter Newell. Fritz, janitor's kid, sets off rocket in basement of apartment house; an ingenious hole punched through every page traces course of rocket. 22 duotone drawings, verses. 48pp. 6⅞ x 8⅜. 22044-3 Pa. $1.50

PECK'S BAD BOY AND HIS PA, George W. Peck. Complete double-volume of great American childhood classic. Hennery's ingenious pranks against outraged pomposity of pa and the grocery man. 97 illustrations. Introduction by E.F. Bleiler. 347pp. 20497-9 Pa. $2.50

THE TALE OF PETER RABBIT, Beatrix Potter. The inimitable Peter's terrifying adventure in Mr. McGregor's garden, with all 27 wonderful, full-color Potter illustrations. 55pp. 4¼ x 5½. USO 22827-4 Pa. $1.00

THE TALE OF MRS. TIGGY-WINKLE, Beatrix Potter. Your child will love this story about a very special hedgehog and all 27 wonderful, full-color Potter illustrations. 57pp. 4¼ x 5½. USO 20546-0 Pa. $1.00

THE TALE OF BENJAMIN BUNNY, Beatrix Potter. Peter Rabbit's cousin coaxes him back into Mr. McGregor's garden for a whole new set of adventures. A favorite with children. All 27 full-color illustrations. 59pp. 4¼ x 5½. USO 21102-9 Pa. $1.00

THE MERRY ADVENTURES OF ROBIN HOOD, Howard Pyle. Facsimile of original (1883) edition, finest modern version of English outlaw's adventures. 23 illustrations by Pyle. 296pp. 6½ x 9¼. 22043-5 Pa. $2.75

TWO LITTLE SAVAGES, Ernest Thompson Seton. Adventures of two boys who lived as Indians; explaining Indian ways, woodlore, pioneer methods. 293 illustrations. 286pp. 20985-7 Pa. $3.00

HOUDINI ON MAGIC, Harold Houdini. Edited by Walter Gibson, Morris N. Young. How he escaped; exposés of fake spiritualists; instructions for eye-catching tricks; other fascinating material by and about greatest magician. 155 illustrations. 280pp. 20384-0 Pa. $2.50

HANDBOOK OF THE NUTRITIONAL CONTENTS OF FOOD, U.S. Dept. of Agriculture. Largest, most detailed source of food nutrition information ever prepared. Two mammoth tables: one measuring nutrients in 100 grams of edible portion; the other, in edible portion of 1 pound as purchased. Originally titled Composition of Foods. 190pp. 9 x 12. 21342-0 Pa. $4.00

COMPLETE GUIDE TO HOME CANNING, PRESERVING AND FREEZING, U.S. Dept. of Agriculture. Seven basic manuals with full instructions for jams and jellies; pickles and relishes; canning fruits, vegetables, meat; freezing anything. Really good recipes, exact instructions for optimal results. Save a fortune in food. 156 illustrations. 214pp. 6⅛ x 9¼. 22911-4 Pa. $2.50

THE BREAD TRAY, Louis P. De Gouy. Nearly every bread the cook could buy or make: bread sticks of Italy, fruit breads of Greece, glazed rolls of Vienna, everything from corn pone to croissants. Over 500 recipes altogether. including buns, rolls, muffins, scones, and more. 463pp. 23000-7 Pa. $3.50

CREATIVE HAMBURGER COOKERY, Louis P. De Gouy. 182 unusual recipes for casseroles, meat loaves and hamburgers that turn inexpensive ground meat into memorable main dishes: Arizona chili burgers, burger tamale pie, burger stew, burger corn loaf, burger wine loaf, and more. 120pp. 23001-5 Pa. $1.75

LONG ISLAND SEAFOOD COOKBOOK, J. George Frederick and Jean Joyce. Probably the best American seafood cookbook. Hundreds of recipes. 40 gourmet sauces, 123 recipes using oysters alone! All varieties of fish and seafood amply represented. 324pp. 22677-8 Pa. $3.00

THE EPICUREAN: A COMPLETE TREATISE OF ANALYTICAL AND PRACTICAL STUDIES IN THE CULINARY ART, Charles Ranhofer. Great modern classic. 3,500 recipes from master chef of Delmonico's, turn-of-the-century America's best restaurant. Also explained, many techniques known only to professional chefs. 775 illustrations. 1183pp. 6⅝ x 10. 22680-8 Clothbd. $17.50

THE AMERICAN WINE COOK BOOK, Ted Hatch. Over 700 recipes: old favorites livened up with wine plus many more: Czech fish soup, quince soup, sauce Perigueux, shrimp shortcake, filets Stroganoff, cordon bleu goulash, jambonneau, wine fruit cake, more. 314pp. 22796-0 Pa. $2.50

DELICIOUS VEGETARIAN COOKING, Ivan Baker. Close to 500 delicious and varied recipes: soups, main course dishes (pea, bean, lentil, cheese, vegetable, pasta, and egg dishes), savories, stews, whole-wheat breads and cakes, more. 168pp. USO 22834-7 Pa. $1.75

CATALOGUE OF DOVER BOOKS